NATIVE AMERICAN WISDOM

A Comprehensive Guide to the History, Culture & Herbal Practices of Indigenous Americans

HISTORY BROUGHT ALIVE

FREE BONUS FROM HBA: EBOOK BUNDLE

Greetings!

First of all, thank you for reading our books. As fellow passionate readers of History and Mythology, we aim to create the very best books for our readers.

Now, we invite you to join our VIP list. As a welcome gift, we offer the History & Mythology Ebook Bundle below for free. Plus you can be the first to receive new books and exclusives! Remember it's 100% free to join.

Simply scan the QR code to join.

THE VIKINGS
GREEK MYTHOLOGY
NORSE MYTHOLOGY
ROMAN EMPIRE
FREE
DOWNLOAD

CONTENTS

NATIVE AMERICAN HERBALISM: IMPROVE YOUR HEALTH, WELLNESS & VITALITY WITH INDIGENOUS HEALING PRACTICES, MEDICINAL PLANTS, NATURAL HERBS, & HERBALIST REMEDIES

NATIVE AMERICAN HISTORY

Accurate & Comprehensive History, Origins, Culture, Tribes, Legends, Mythology, Wars, Stories & More of The Native Indigenous Americans

HISTORY BROUGHT ALIVE

INTRODUCTION

We are fortunate to live in a modern world with information at our fingertips. With all the information available, it's surprising that when it comes to history topics, including the history of Indigenous Peoples in North America, the resources we find tend to be dry and dull like an old-fashioned encyclopedia. Frequently, history books are written by academics for academics and are too nuanced or in-depth to capture the curiosity and imagination of the average reader. These history books fail to pique the interests of average people who want to learn more about historical times or cultures.

History Brought Alive strives to deliver history books that everyone will enjoy. History Brought Alive offers a series of history books thoughtfully inspired by you, our reader, and all the people of the world. In this book, we will educate you about the history of Indigenous Peoples in North America. We believe that we build more understanding and respect through education and awareness. We do this by offering you a book that is well researched and laid out in a way that flows from one topic to the next to build on what you're learning. We say "goodbye!" to old-school history texts and invite you to enjoy learning and expanding your knowledge on this subject.

Multiculturalism

Another incredible feature of this modern-day world is the

extent to which accessible travel and globalism have brought us all together. We now live in a multicultural world and interact with many more cultures and people than ever before. For this reason, it is essential to learn more about cultures beyond your own. Education builds awareness, understanding, and compassion. Learning more about different cultures and histories is a part of being a good global citizen. Whether you travel frequently or not you probably come into contact with dozens of people of various backgrounds and cultures every day without even realizing it. Learning more about history allows for deeper conversations and understanding of everyone around us. It helps us to be more inclusive and less judgmental when it comes to other cultures.

Era of Reconciliation

At this point in history, it is essential for people to learn more about the history of Indigenous Peoples in North America. Tragically, and for far too long, the various Indigenous cultures in North America have been systematically eliminated, misrepresented, and misunderstood. Poor historical treatment has led to deeply seeded trauma and adverse economic and health outcomes for many Indigenous People. Recently, there has been more information available about the mistreatment of Indigenous People and the intergenerational effects of that mistreatment. Some of the adverse impacts for people of Indigenous descent include higher rates of poverty, children in state care, shorter life expectancy, and higher rates of drug or alcohol substance use disorders. These outcomes are related to the experience of trauma and poverty and become compounded with multi-generational trauma, such as experienced by most Indigenous People.

We are at the brink of a decisive turning point in North

America, where people can share an Indigenous perspective more broadly through social media and other alternative news sources and narratives. The broader ability to share information has opened many more eyes to the racism, injustices, and challenges Indigenous people have faced since colonialism. It is a point at which we all need to take responsibility to become educated about the long history and diverse cultures of Native Americans and begin to develop an awareness of how colonialism and continued colonial practices affect present-day Indigenous people and culture.

We hope that everyone may support the future generations of Indigenous Peoples in healing and grow into a beautiful new Era through education and understanding. This book is an excellent starting place for your learning journey and understanding the complex history of Indigenous Peoples in North America. Begin here with "The Complete History of Indigenous Peoples in North America" but we urge you to dive deeper into the local history in the area you inhabit. We would also encourage you to seek out Indigenous-owned and curated businesses, shops, apparel, art, and literature in your local area. Each part of the continent is home to a distinct and diverse Native American nation or tribe, so it's a good idea to learn about the history specific to your area to understand the people around you better.

Land Acknowledgement

We wish to acknowledge and honor that we live and work on the ancestral lands and traditional territories of many Indigenous tribes and nations across North America.

As we will discuss in detail later in this book, everything changed for Indigenous Peoples when European colonizers arrived to settle in North America. Before colonization, Indigenous peoples lived sustainably with the environment and had no reason to change their traditional ways of life for thousands of years. Only when colonizers arrived in present-day North America, was their sustainable way of life disrupted.

The colonizers destroyed the subtle balance that existed between humans and the environment for tens of thousands of years. Colonizers were ignorant and didn't understand the connection that Indigenous Peoples had to the land and how they relied on it to live nor how it was tied to their beliefs and traditions. As Indigenous Peoples were forced off of traditional territories or onto small reserves of land in the territories, they could no longer live sustainably, and many poor outcomes have resulted.

At the same time, as Indigenous people were being negatively affected by displacement and limited land usage due to colonialism, the settling colonizers were directly profiting from it. The culture clash between greedy colonizers and holistic Indigenous peoples caused a drastic imbalance in the power dynamic. Today, this still affects the relationship between settler descendants and Indigenous people in North America. It took a few hundred years before people in the dominant culture started to clearly see how much colonialism has affected Indigenous people.

At this point in history in North America, more and more people are showing respect by acknowledging the heritage of the land and of the people who lived on it for thousands of years. This new practice is called Land Acknowledgement. It is now common to hear or read a Land Acknowledgement at the beginning of many events and gatherings, on business websites, or through literature from non-profit organizations. Land Acknowledgements serve to honor true history by recognizing the historical fact that European colonizers stole

Indigenous Peoples' land in North America.

CHAPTER 1
A BRIEF HISTORY OF HUMANITY

Before we dig into the vibrant history of the Indigenous Peoples in North America, we will take a trip back in time, about 2 million years. It would be hard to begin the story of Indigenous Peoples without first briefly touching on the history of the evolution of humans and where we first appeared, and how and when we migrated across the globe. This way, we can put into context the arrival of Indigenous Peoples in North America. Recounting the evolution of humanity is also a way to remind us all that we are a united race with a common ancestral beginning. Since the dawn of humanity, people have dispersed into different parts of the world; that dispersion has led to so many diverse and beautiful human cultures.

Prehistoric Human Ancestors

Although scientists are still unsure exactly when and where humans first came into existence, the earliest human ancestor remains were discovered in the country now known as Kenya and are dated to be nearly 3 million years old. Every time another ancient prehistoric artifact is uncovered, it brings new information and insight. Because of this, we will likely never know for sure the precise origins of the human race.

For some of us, the idea of our own species' origin

remaining a mystery is frustrating or confusing; for many scientists, this is what makes anthropology and paleontology so interesting. Scientists and anthropologists who work on these types of excavations are constantly motivated by the quest to solve the mystery and uncover the next fossil that will unlock another aspect of ancient humanity and fill in some gaps of our origin story.

Because it wasn't until about 5,000 years ago that humans began to maintain records, other than verbally communicated memories and information, we rely heavily on the information discovered from fossils and ancient relics. Anthropologists use that information to continuously piece together an idea of how and where ancient humans lived, what they ate, and where they traveled.

Modern-day humans are a part of the Hominini family of primates, which the Merriam-Webster dictionary defines as: "any of a taxonomic tribe (Hominini) of hominids that includes recent humans together with extinct ancestral related forms." Due to the availability of genetic testing from ancient samples, we know there were several species of archaic humans, such as Neanderthals and different types of hominids. It is also now known that many of these species were close enough to mate and produce offspring and continue human evolution in that way. Our species, the Homo sapiens, directly evolved from the Homo erectus, which coupled with other species such as Neanderthals. The outcome of all this means that we modern-day humans have genes from many now-extinct human species.

Each of these human ancestors had distinct features, abilities, and lifestyles; they each played a part in forming our modern species of humans, the Homo sapiens. The earliest remains and evidence of the existence of Homo sapiens specifically, were also found in the eastern region of Africa near Kenya and Ethiopia and dated from around 315,000 years ago. Of all the types of hominids that existed over millions of years, modern humans or Homo sapiens are the only ones that remain. Our closest living relatives who still exist are primates such as gorillas and orangutans.

Migration of Prehistoric Humans

The geographical world and environment of the ancient hominid species were vastly different from our world today, including the physical placement and locations of the continents and land on Earth. Scientists currently believe that when hominids were first evolving, all the continents on the planet were bunched together into one giant landmass called Pangea. The connected landmass of Pangea eventually separated and moved into the locations we have today by the slow and continuous drifting of the continental plates. The continental plates continue to drift to this day at a prolonged and imperceptible rate. This continental drift created many of the beautiful natural features in our world today, including the collision of tectonic plates that caused mountains to form.

Evidence suggests that human ancestors existed on the continent now known as Africa for about 1 million years before migrating eastward through present-day Europe and beyond to what is now known as Asia. The oldest hominid remains in Asia are a pair of teeth found in China, dating from about 1.7 million years ago. There has been other evidence of Homo erectus found in China that dates back even further. It's safe for scientists to say that our ancient ancestors had made it from Africa to Asia about 2 million years ago.

Remains and artifacts in Europe date the arrival and habitation of hominids in that area around 600,000 years ago. However, it is not believed that Homo sapiens were in

Europe until about 45,000 years ago. Anthropologists do not know why Homo sapiens took so long to inhabit Europe. There is plenty of evidence that Homo sapiens had already been inhabiting Asia, which would have required them to pass through Europe from Africa to Asia, long before they finally inhabited Europe. Exactly when and why Homo sapiens finally populated Europe is a question that will require further archaeological discoveries to be able to answer.

CHAPTER 2

THEORIES OF ARRIVAL IN THE AMERICAS

Human arrival in the Americas is relatively recent compared with the rest of human evolution and migration history. Exactly when and how it happened remains somewhat mysterious, with ongoing discoveries changing the former theories and bringing up new likely scenarios of how the first Indigenous peoples may have arrived in the Americas. It is presumed that different groups of humans may have made their way here at other times and in different ways. This chapter will share the main western scientific theories of how people made their way to the Americas—followed in the next chapter by Indigenous origin stories and views.

The Bering Land Bridge Theory

Perhaps you are familiar with the Bering Land Bridge theory of how humans first migrated from Asia to the Americas. Until a few short years ago, when paleontologists discovered new artifacts, it was commonly believed and taught that humans first made their way to North America by following and hunting big game animals across a span of land that once existed between Alaska and Siberia. The previous evidence suggested that this happened about 13,000-14,000 years ago, where the Bering Strait exists today.

It was believed in this theory that as the ice receded after the Ice Age, a group of humans who had been inhabiting eastern Asia were able to cross a land bridge that became accessible for migration by foot. Although anthropologists widely accepted the Bering Land Bridge theory for many years, there always remained questions about whether it was possible given the age of the artifacts and the dates of the ice receding. It seemed that the evidence of humans in America was older than the time when the Bering Land Bridge would have been clear of ice. For that reason, scientists had been left seeking more information on when and how Indigenous People made their way to North America.

Beringia

It appears that what was called the Bering Land Bridge was a sizable continent-sized landmass now called Beringia. Twenty-five thousand years ago, that area was a massive and rare piece of dry land during the Ice Age. Due to unique natural conditions, it miraculously remained clear of ice despite the arctic conditions that enveloped the entire Earth at that time. Throughout the Ice Age, most of the Earth's water was in the form of glaciers and ice, making the world's water level much lower than it is today, allowing for more coastal land to be exposed. Because of that, Beringia connected the eastern side of Asia from Siberia to the western side of North America in the Alaska region.

A few pieces of land in the Bering Strait remain above water, and there has been evidence of mammoth bones and other fossils uncovered on those islands that suggest that humans were present there at least 25,000 years ago, not 14,000 as previously believed. These initial discoveries led scientists to question the timing of our human ancestors' first arrival in North America. As scientists broadened their search for artifacts into Alaska and Siberia, they have collected evidence of ancient human activity on either side of the Bering

Strait. In Alaska, the artifacts are 20,000-25,000 years old, and on the Siberia side, they are over 35,000 years. Some evidence suggests that 25,000 years ago, the ice would not have been receded enough to be passable from Siberia to Alaska via the Bering Land Bridge; leading some scientists to believe that it is possible that Indigenous people were in that area for much, much longer than previously believed. This mounting evidence points to the fact that ancient humans actually inhabited that entire area for quite a long time. It is now recognized as having been an exceptional place and time in both history and geography, a unique place where the environment put humans' ability to survive to the test in extremely harsh conditions.

These are important discoveries that have altered the former theories of timeline and mode of the arrival of the Indigenous People in North America. Scientists believe the answers to many of these questions are encapsulated deep beneath the Bering Sea, a buried treasure from our ancestors.

The Clovis Culture People

For decades, the dominant theory of human population in the Americas was that ancient people crossed the Bering Land Bridge about 13,000 years ago. The theory held that the Indigenous People gradually migrated south from the Canadian far north down to South America. In the 1920s, archaeological remains of tools and bones found in Clovis, New Mexico, gave anthropologists the first views of the type of culture and lifestyle these Indigenous people had. They named this culture and the people after the site where the artifacts were discovered, the Clovis people. It was found that the Clovis people migrated to many parts of the Americas, and it was believed for a long time that they were the original gene source in North and South America.

Since the advancements and availability of genetic testing on ancient bone artifacts, scientists have been able to piece together more of the puzzle of the history of the Indigenous population of the Americas. However, some genetic test results have also raised questions about unknown gene sources linked to a previously unknown group of people who are not genetically related to the Clovis people. Another shocking discovery is that the gene lineage associated with the Clovis people seems to have ended abruptly around 9,000 years ago. This type of information and the insights that scientists have gained from it would never have been possible until a few years ago as technology advanced.

Here is an excerpt from the article Clovis People Spread to Central and South America, then Vanished, which explains the impact of genetic testing and how it has informed anthropologists and altered views about ancient humans in North America:

Ancient DNA offered a new way to look at the question. Reich and his collaborators compared ancient peoples' genes from sites in Central and South America to genes from a Clovis-linked individual who lived in today's Montana between 12,700 and 12,900 years ago. There was a clear match between the Montana individual's genes and the three oldest genetic samples in the new study, which came from Chile, Brazil, and Belize. [...]

But then came the surprise. The great majority of the other individuals analyzed, who lived from Belize to Patagonia between 3,000 and 9,000 years ago, belonged to a different genetic lineage. The data imply that a population separate and distinct from the Clovis group also swept south from North America, largely replacing the Clovis-linked lineages. Their identity? Still a mystery. Reich is hoping that archeologists can help solve the puzzle, in combination with additional ancient DNA data. "That's an exciting part of the active dialogue between these two fields," he says. (Reich, 2018, para 7-9)

Another plot-twisting discovery came from testing samples that had been collected from across the Americas. During the testing process, scientists discovered a unique and distinct ancient human DNA from a sample found in South America, which is older than any Clovis DNA samples. This discovery points to the fact that there was or had already been a distinct human population in South America by the time the Clovis people reached it.

It now seems likely that the Clovis people migrating through the Bering Land Bridge is one of the ways that prehistoric humans came to North America, but it is unlikely that it is the only way. So, once again, as anthropologists gain more information, they are left with more questions. There is still no connection between the older South American DNA samples with any other known people, but scientists are hoping that one day a new sample will turn up to provide an answer.

The Kelp Highway

For many decades, anthropologists have considered the idea of prehistoric humans making their way to the Americas via sea as opposed to land. Until a few years ago, this idea was not held with much esteem but viewed as a peripheral possibility. More recently, due to the mounting evidence that proves that humans did inhabit the Americas before the Bering Land Bridge would have been clear of ice to facilitate passage, the idea of marine travel is becoming more popular. Many anthropologists now regard the theory of prehistoric maritime travel as the most likely way our ancient ancestors could have traveled when they did.

Although maritime travel now appears to be the most plausible way the very first humans arrived in the Americas, there is still very little known about how they did it. Anthropologists have long known that ancient humans were capable of maritime travel and had populated other regions, for example, Australia, in that way.

Maritime scientists, called paleoecologists, study ancient environments and the relationship between the environment and the people, plants, and animals of that time. They are investigating the Pacific coastline to better understand the type of marine and coastal environment that the ancient seafarers may have been navigating. Because the water level in the ocean was considerably lower at the time the ancient humans were traveling, it is believed that much of the evidence of their maritime travel and coastal lifestyle in the Americas is now underwater and most likely washed away or eroded. Anthropologists now view the submersion of the prehistoric coastline and the resulting loss of artifacts as a potential reason why they had not seriously evaluated this Kelp Highway Theory. Because of the inability to access the prehistoric coast, scientists are somewhat discouraged about the prospects of uncovering artifacts that can help fill in the details about the prehistoric maritime migration.

Islands along the pacific rim of North America appear to offer the most significant source of hope for paleontologists seeking to uncover clues about the maritime journey. It is on the small north pacific islands where a few specialized paleontologists have focused on locating ancient fossils. When these scientists started their work, the initial goal was to deepen the knowledge of the history of the local Indigenous Peoples of the area. They developed new techniques and skills to recover marine and coastal artifacts.

Over the past few years, as more information confirms the validity of the Kelp Highway Theory, it became clear that the best place to look for artifacts from the Indigenous People's migration is on the islands in the North Pacific. Although, as previously mentioned, because the water level has risen, the geography of the Pacific coastline is quite different now than it was over 20,000 years ago when those brave first humans traveled the icy Pacific to the Americas.

However, paleoecologists have discovered another fascinating factor: The land on the pacific coastline rose, just as a flattened sponge would, once the weight of the nearly two-mile tall glaciers was released. This effect was good news for paleontologists and archaeologists, as it seems that the coastline in that area, unlike some other places, is not so far from what it was when the Indigenous People were making their way to present-day America.

Scientists are also fortunate to have access to the very complex and sophisticated technology that enables them to use aerial imaging to calculate the coastline from 20,000 years ago. This technology helps them identify which islands or coastal areas are more likely to have significant archaeological sites. This technology can streamline the process of site selection and has led to the discovery of hundreds of artifacts that continue to support the possibility of the maritime migration theory.

CHAPTER 3
THE STORY OF THE INDIGENOUS PEOPLE IN THE AMERICANS

Indigenous knowledge has always been passed on verbally from one generation to the next. The Canadian History Museum describes the importance of the Indigenous tradition of oral history sharing in this way:

First Peoples remember their origins through oral histories passed down by elders in each generation.

These narratives describe the creation of the world and how the First Peoples came to live in it. More than legends, they embody a view of how the world fits together, and how human beings should behave in it.

Some oral histories refer to a time before human occupation. Others mark significant geographical, spiritual, and life events that have occurred over the millennia. (n.d. para 1-3)

The stories are sacred, and great attention is given to maintaining the authentic tradition of sharing history in this way. It must be understood and respected that this particular way of recording history is central to Indigenous culture and ways of knowing.

Indigenous Ways of Knowing

Before moving into the various origin stories of the Indigenous Peoples of North America, it is essential to understand that Indigenous ways of knowing are distinct from the concepts of Western knowledge. Unlike the Western view that knowledge must be tested and 'proven' to be validated, Indigenous ways of knowing to encompass a broader affirmation and validity of knowledge from many sources. For this reason, many Indigenous people don't believe in or support the need for scientific evidence to show how the People came to live in North America. It may be hurtful and controversial for many Indigenous People and communities to have Western scientists excavating the land and removing ancestral remains.

So far, the information in this book has been exclusively rooted in Western views of knowledge, including the Western need to 'discover' and 'prove' how the Indigenous Peoples arrived in North America. A perspective more grounded in Indigenous ways of knowing would recognize that each nation has an origin story passed down since the Indigenous People arrived in North America.

In some Indigenous cultures, North America is called Turtle Island. These origin stories, recorded and transmitted orally, are the true and valid history of how each nation came to live on Turtle Island. It must also be noted that there are many Indigenous Nations on Turtle Island with many distinct histories and unique cultural characteristics. There does not exist one Indigenous history or one specific Indigenous way of knowing; each Indigenous nation is different from another to varying degrees. Some Indigenous Nations may appear to have overlapping values and cultures, others may not.

Characteristics of Indigenous ways of knowing that are

central to many Indigenous Nation cultures include holistic views of the world in which we live. A holistic view considers the many relationships that exist between an individual and their family, their community, their environment, the food they eat, the places they go, and how they might interact with those places. Many Indigenous cultures emphasize a natural awareness and consider not just an individual but the individual in relation to others and the land. Generally, the effects of one's actions upon others and the land are more recognized and valued in Indigenous cultures than Western cultures. We can also describe that worldview as relational.

In Western cultures, values and actions often revolve around the idea of capitalism so that each person should try to get as much as possible for themselves, regardless of the outcome it might have on other people or the land and environment. It is generally considered valid, understandable, and even admirable for an individual in Western culture to hoard wealth and resources away from others.

The radically opposing fundamental worldviews, values, and ways of knowing between Indigenous Peoples and the Western European colonizers led to catastrophic outcomes for Indigenous People on Turtle Island. Indigenous Peoples had not encountered the capitalist mindset before colonialism. Having no understanding that such ways of being were even possible, they were taken advantage of in that regard.

Themes of Indigenous Creation Stories

Storytelling, especially the sharing of creation stories, is a cornerstone of nearly all Indigenous cultures. It is how information and wisdom pass from one generation to the next. Storytellers are deeply respected and honored in most Indigenous communities as they maintain and share knowledge and history. It can't be overemphasized how much the practice of this oral history tradition means to Indigenous culture and ways of knowing. It should be regarded as sacred and an equally valid way of learning and sharing information.

For the most part, each Indigenous nation has its own creation story, describing how humans came to exist. Many creation stories also explain how the land and animals came into existence, but in many others, the land was already there when humans were.

Although each Nation has its own creation story, there are common themes in many of them. Animals tend to feature heavily in many creation stories. In some stories, an animal is the creator of humans. For example, in the Salinan creation story, the bald eagle is the creator of the humans and makes them first out of clay. Certain animals are common, showing up as a creator or central character in several creation stories. For example, the crow, bald eagle, coyote, horse, and bear appear in many creation stories.

Another common theme in Indigenous creation stories is the need to find a balance, or how the People found peace. In nearly all the creation stories, humans come to land after the animals. In some creation stories, once humans were created, they disrupted a natural balance of what came before them. In other stories, they were out of balance in their attitudes and actions and learning through experience that greed and conflict are not helpful. In their process of experiential growth, humans learned that working cooperatively with each other and with the animals and environment is the most harmonious and peaceful way of being.

Natural disasters are also a common element in some creation stories. It seems that most of the time when natural disasters are a part of creation stories, it is to learn to respect the elements and nature or to overcome a time of turmoil to find peace through cooperation. Many Indigenous stories (other than creation stories) were also used to document and recount severe natural disasters. It often seems these disasters are floods, and there is a deep respect for water as it is viewed as the lifeblood of Mother Earth; it is revered for being so powerful.

Anishinaabe Creation Story

Here is an Anishinaabe Peoples' Creation story. It is a beautiful example of the types of themes are seen in many Indigenous creation stories including the Creator, or Great Spirit called 'Gitchi Manitou', the personification of Earth as a mother being, the use of the four directions to represent different parts that make up a whole, the mention of the importance and power of water, and the union of 'man' with Earth and with the animals.

When the Earth was young, it had a family. The Moon is called Grandmother, and the Sun is called Grandfather. This family is the basis of all creation in the universe. This family was created by Gitchi Manitou, the Creator. Earth is said to be a woman. She preceded man and her name is Mother Earth because all living things live from her gifts. Water is her lifeblood. It flows through her, nourishes her, and purifies her.

Mother Earth was given Four Sacred Directions – North, South, East, and West. Each direction contributes a vital part of her wholeness. Each direction and all things on Mother Earth have physical powers and spiritual powers.

When she was young, Mother Earth was filled with beauty. The Creator sent his singers in the form of birds to carry the seeds of life to all of the Four Sacred Directions. Life was spread across the land. The Creator placed the swimming creatures in the water. He placed the crawling things and the four-legged animals on the land. He gave life to all the plants and insects of the world. All parts of life lived in harmony with each other on Mother Earth.

Gitchi Manitou took the four parts of Mother Earth and blew them into a Sacred Megis Shell. From the union of the Four Sacred Elements and his breath, a man was created. It is said that Gitchi Manitou then lowered the man to the Earth. Thus, the man was the last form of life to be placed on Earth. From this Original Man came the Anishinaabe people. This man was created in the image of Gitchi Manitou. Man was part of Mother Earth. He lived in a brotherhood with all life that surrounded him. (Parks Canada Agency, 2018, para 1-4)

CHAPTER 4

THE INDIGENOUS RELATIONSHIP WITH THE LAND

Indigenous cultures, although each unique, hold a completely different view of land use and the human relationship with the land than western colonists. Pre-colonization, the concept of ownership never existed in Indigenous cultures. Before the Europeans arrived in the Americas, the land was not divided into states. In pre-contact America, there were no borders or precise measurements of land, which was far different from how it is today. For this reason, many Indigenous people and some non-Indigenous people do not recognize or use the colonial names for places.

The Indigenous views of land use and relationship are very different from how the European settlers viewed land ownership and usage; and very different from how the western colonial descendants continue to view it. Up until roughly 500 years ago, Indigenous nations occupied large territories and sustainably lived off the land. The cultures and lifestyles of each nation were shaped by the environment and geography of the land they occupied. The traditional Indigenous way of life was a delicate and complex relationship between the land and the people that was symbiotic and inextricable.

Indigenous Peoples of the pre-contact era did not

25

conceptualize land ownership, currencies such as money, and certainly not land as "real-estate." The Indigenous view of the land is one of resources and stewardship, of living off as well as with the land in a natural way. The Indigenous Peoples recognized that Mother Earth supplied them with all that was needed to live well. They also realized that it was necessary to steward and foster Mother Earth's ability to provide. Indigenous people commonly knew that nature and the resources from it must be respected and used only as needed and in moderation; otherwise, Mother Earth may not be able to continue to provide it. This profound wisdom was how Indigenous Nations were able to live sustainably since time immemorial. Because the tradition was to take only as much as was needed and value what was being used as a life-giving offering, the Indigenous Peoples didn't need to change their lifestyle or seek more resources. They were able to responsibly manage the land and their use of resources to live comfortably.

The traditional Indigenous way of life was utterly unknown and uninterpretable to the European settlers' view of Earth and natural resources. Europeans had a long history of property and resource ownership. Before Europeans landed in the Americas, they already had a long history of profiting off basic human necessities. In their culture, it was considered morally correct to hoard food and shelter and then to let people die because they could not access those basic necessities, even though the necessities did exist plentifully. As a result of the European beliefs that land and resources were commodities, combined with their seemingly insatiable desire to consume and hoard more resources, Europeans were forced to continually seek out additional resources via colonialism. Sadly, as a result of colonialism, many common so-called European moral beliefs, such as the use of land and resources as commodities, have increased across the globe.

Indigenous Territories

It's hard to clearly describe the traditional territories of the Indigenous Nations in the Americas because they were not necessarily clearly defined boundaries as we are accustomed to seeing today. The territories of many Nations are somewhat complex as many of the boundaries were porous, and the territories were overlapping. Some Indigenous Nations worked together in close relationships, while others had more firm boundaries between them.

Here is a non-exhaustive list of the traditional territories.

The far north of North America is the traditional territory of many Indigenous Nations. Given the ability to live in balance with some of the harshest conditions on the planet, it is safe to say that these are some of the strongest and most robust people in the world. From west to east, the nations that occupy this land are Inupiat, Kuskokwim, Eyak, Tlingit, Koyukon, Teslin Tlingit, Dene, Beaver, Tanana, Got'ine, Dënéndeh, Métis, Gwich'in Nành, Inuvialuit, Inuit, Naskapi, Inughuit Nunaat, and Kalaallit Nunaat.

Still in the north of the continent but descending into the more densely populated parallels, where seasons are distinct, yet more forgiving than in the far north, are the territories of Haida, Coast Salish, Okanagan, Syilx, Wet'suwet'en, Dënédeh, Yekooche, Cree, Stoney, Métis, Plains Cree, Assiniboine, Anishinabewaki, Wabanaki, Mi'kmaq'i, and the former Beothuk people. In this region of the continent, average temperatures are warmer, and growing seasons are longer. At this level of the globe, there is a drastic change in the climates as we move from the wet and temperate west coast, through the rugged mountains, across the extremes of the prairies, into densely forested woodland, and back out to coastal conditions on the east side of the continent. The diversity of the environments of the territories is reflected in the diversity of the Indigenous Nations that occupy them.

Moving down toward the present-day border between the United States and Canada are the territories of these Indigenous Nations: Quatsino, Squamish, Salish, Makah, Nisquali, Smish, K'ómoks, Yakama, Spokane, Chelan, Cheyenne, Niitsítapi (Blackfoot), Anishinabewaki, Mississauga, and Kanien'kehá:ka (Mohawk).

From west to east at the mid-latitudes in the United States are the traditional lands of Kalapuya, Siletz, Lakota, Dakota, Chinook, Pomo, Yuki, Yahooskin, Numu, Newe, Nimiipuu (Nez Perce), Shoshone-Bannock, Eastern Shoshone, and Cheyenne.

In the Southern United States, roughly from west to east are the territories Confederation of the Siletz Indians, Numu, Newe, Shoshone-Bannock, Pueblos, Comanche, Apache, Peoria, Osage, Shawnee, Tsalaguwetiyi, Creek, Choctaw, and Lumbee.

In present-day Mexico, we find the traditional territory of these Indigenous Nations and civilizations: Cocohimí, Guaycura, Jojocobas, Tepehuán, Coahuiltecan, Gwachichi, Mexihcah, Nahua, Zapoteco, Aztec, Maya, Chorotega, and Rama.

CHAPTER 5

TRADITIONAL LIFESTYLES AND CULTURES

The geographic location and environment that each Indigenous Nation historically occupied shaped the lifestyle and resulting culture. Although all Indigenous Nations are distinct, there do tend to be more overlapping similarities between cultures of Indigenous Nations that evolved to survive in similar environments. Geographically close groups tend to share cultural similarities because a sizable part of traditional Indigenous lifestyles revolved around procuring the necessities for survival, such as hunting and gathering practices, clothing fabrication techniques, types of tools, and housing.

There are also far too many individual nations to list all of them and their unique lifestyles. For this reason, traditional Indigenous lifestyles are best described by region rather than by specific nation or group. In the case of an Indigenous nation whose lifestyle and culture was quite different from the regional norms of the area surrounding their territory.

The Inuit Nations of the Far North

Most Indigenous peoples in the far north are Inuit (Inuvialuit) or related to the Inuit culture. Inuit have lived in the Arctic for over 4,000 years and adapted specialized skills for surviving there.

Being efficient is probably more important in the harsh conditions of the Arctic than anywhere else in the world. Each season in the far north is distinct and must be used in its own way to maximize productivity. Because many foods or items were only available seasonally, the Inuk spent much of the year preparing for the long, intense winters; that preparation was key to survival.

The traditional lifestyle of the Inuit was semi-nomadic. The community groups migrated a few times a year with the change of the seasons. Each community group traveled to the same specific and known sites year after year to hunt, gather, fish, or harvest other necessary items.

The times for migration would vary from one year to the next, depending on the weather and the animals; this is one example of the ways and reasons that most Indigenous Nations are so intertwined with nature. The traditional way of the Inuit was to take the cue from the environment and act in response to that, moving in step with the natural world.

Traditionally, caribou were a substantial part of the Inuit subsistence and would influence migration for the hunting pods twice a year. The massive caribou herd would migrate north in the spring and south in the fall. During those times of the year, when the caribou were gathered in such large numbers, it was easier for the Inuks to hunt them successfully. It was important for the Inuit groups to have their camps established in strategic locations to make hunting and processing the caribou most efficient in the spring and fall. The fall caribou hunting season was crucial as it provided a large portion of the food and fur that the Inuit groups would need to use for survival throughout the winter. If something went wrong during the fall hunt, it might mean a lack of food for winter, and the result of that could potentially be deadly.

Spring and fall camps consisted of tent-like shelter structures made from small logs as posts and animal skins as the sides and roof. These structures could be transported and reassembled relatively quickly, making them ideal for the needs of the Inuit groups as they migrated with changing seasons.

In the winter months, Inuks traditionally built shelters out of ice blocks. Because of the size and design of the ice shelters, they could even have fires inside the ice homes, called igloos. The igloo walls were many inches thick and provided a solid protective structure that was well insulated all winter long.

The Inuit hunted seals for meat and fur during the winter months. It was customary for all Indigenous Nations to use all parts of the animals they hunted. The meat for eating, the skin for clothing, and the bones for tools or jewelry. Nothing was wasted, and animals were not hunted unless needed and entirely used.

For travel in the winter months and to transport items over snow, Inuks designed and crafted sleds. They used bones or branches with animal hides to build multi-functional sleds that were light and durable. The Inuit would also use domesticated dogs to help pull the sleds.

Winter is very long and very dark in the Arctic region. Inuks spent a lot of time during winter in igloos with their family. Traditionally winter was when stories, craftwork, games, songs, and dances were passed on to younger generations; and practiced for fun to keep occupied over the many months of winter.

When the days got longer and the snow began to melt, the Inuit knew it was time to start to prepare for the spring. For each hunting group, this meant migrating to their specific spring camp location in hopes of harvesting as many caribou as needed while the massive herds migrate north for the summer. After a long winter of living off mainly seal meat, spring was likely an exciting time to begin to diversify the diet once again, starting with the caribou, then with fresh plants and berries as they become available throughout the summer.

For the most part, Inuit lived near the ocean year-round, although in the Arctic, for much of the year, the ice was so thick, you would hardly be able to tell there was ocean beneath it or nearby. They relied heavily on what the sea provided for food and ate primarily meat and fish year-round.

Traditionally, many of the Inuit family hunting groups camped near an accessible coast in the summer months. They designed and used kayaks to travel long distances over water very efficiently. Inuks were master anglers, hunting and catching all types of edible and valuable marine animals, even as large as whales.

Inuit clothing was made from animal furs and hides. Seemingly miraculously, but as in all other aspects of life, Mother Earth provided the People with all that was necessary for survival in the Arctic climate. The furs of the animals they hunted for food were exactly what was needed to protect them against the harsh elements of the far north. Seal fur made a perfectly warm and waterproof material that Inuks traditionally used for mittens, boots, coats, baby wraps, and more.

The people themselves tended to be of small stature and naturally very fit and strong due to lifestyle. Their bodies would adapt and change with the seasons, as they were more active in certain months and had more food to live off in those months as well. Just like everything else in the natural environment, they themselves changed naturally over the course of the year. The Inuk's facial features, hair, and skin resemble the typical features of many Asiatic-related groups.

The traditional Inuit culture was very communal and interconnected. Most of the community groups consisted of family pods that included a mother, father, children, often an adopted child or niece or nephew, and relatives such as siblings who were not married, and sometimes the grandparents as well, especially as they aged. A few related family pods would often group together in a commune to share work and life.

Inuit always worked together to accomplish tasks and keep the community fed, clothed, and housed; they shared the labor and the fruits unilaterally. Even though everyone had unique strengths or talents, each individual offered their abilities to serve the group and shared equally in the resources and outcomes. Working together in that way was essential to survival in the harsh conditions of the territory they occupied; no one could survive in the Arctic on their own. At some point, everyone in the group would need to receive and offer help.

The Inuit created a deep connection to nature by being in tune with environmental changes in their natural habitat and living organically in response. Traditionally, the Inuit viewed themselves as one with Mother Earth, not as humans separate from it. This connection with the Earth is a fundamental and distinguishing feature of traditional Indigenous culture that differs drastically from European settler worldviews. The colonizers lacked an understanding of the relationship between the Indigenous Nations and the land. This lack of knowledge led colonizers to make poor and arrogant choices regarding the treatment of the humans and the land they encountered in the Americas, decisions which have led to the extinction of countless species of plants and animals, and even ultimately to climate change.

Post-Colonial Contact in the Arctic

At the time of contact in the 1500s, on the East Coast of North America, Indigenous Peoples were living almost exactly the way they had been for, in some cases, over 10 thousand years. European contact changed that completely. The specific effects of contact and colonialism were different for Nations in other parts of the continent. However, over time the European settlers completely altered the Indigenous way of life to the point that it no longer functioned for survival, let alone in the beautiful symbiotic and sustainable way of life that it had provided for time immemorial.

Inuit contact with Europeans started in the east, as Europeans arrived from that direction and then progressed westward over the course of 100-150 years. The first Inuit to encounter the Europeans lived in Labrador and encountered explorers first. After the explorers, Inuit contact with settlers slowly increased over time as European settlers sailed north seasonally to hunt whales; the whalers would interact with or trade with Indigenous communities when they did. At first, the contact was relatively minimal and did not significantly alter the Inuit's way of life; they continued to move seasonally and maximize the use of natural resources available in each season.

Over time some Inuks began to travel south in the summer to trade in the settler villages, they exchanged furs for metal tools, blankets, clothing, and other valuable items. It was trading with settlers that slowly altered the way of life for Inuks by introducing new technologies. Although this type of trade seemed unintrusive at first, it was the beginning of the change from exclusively Indigenous ways of living to an ultimately unsustainable European-influenced lifestyle. It also introduced Indigenous Peoples to the European system of values, a capitalist system based on currency, private property ownership, and greed which was utterly different from the Inuit values.

As contact between the two cultures continued to increase, disputes and conflicts between the Inuit and the settlers became more frequent. It was in the 1700s, when more demand for whale fat increased the whaling activity and contact in the Far North, with whalers becoming commonplace in the North over the summer months. Eventually, in the 1800s, whaling activity became year-round in the Arctic, and Inuit communities were continuously in contact with European Settlers.

One of the first detrimental effects of increased contact was the transmission of diseases from the settlers to the Inuit. The Indigenous Peoples in the Americas all suffered greatly as the new illnesses swept through communities killing many.

Another detrimental effect of contact and settlement that impacted the Inuit culture and lifestyle was the over-harvesting of marine animals, such as whales. Although Inuit had lived in the Arctic for time immemorial and had harvested all types of marine animals, including whales, for thousands of years, they had always practiced sustainable and responsible hunting and harvesting techniques. The new settlers and whalers from Europe quickly overharvested the whale population within a matter of several decades. Overharvesting altered the relationship of the Inuit with the land and animals that they had relied upon for generations. As the supply and demand for whale fat diminished, the fur trade experienced an uptick in demand, which brought even more settlers to the arctic searching for pelts for the European fashion industry.

During that time, tensions mounted as culture clashes and misunderstandings led to increasing conflicts between the Inuits and the settlers. Colonizers began to feel the need to assimilate Inuit to the European settlers' culture and lifestyle. They believed it would relieve tensions between the cultures if they could eliminate the traditional cultures and alter the Inuit's way of life to better suit the needs of the growing settler population. Missions were established throughout the North starting in the mid to late 1700s. The missions were used as a school structure to teach Inuit how to read and write in Inuktitut and English. The missionaries also taught the Inuks Christianity with the goal of teaching the Inuks to adopt the new European way of life and leave the traditional Inuit culture behind. In some cases, in hopes of minimizing contact and easing tensions between the raiders and the Indigenous Peoples, the missionaries also took over the trade interactions between the European fur traders and the Indigenous hunters.

Over the course of the 200 years that followed contact, most Inuit were converted to Christianity. The shift to Christianity changed the fundamental views that shaped the culture and lifestyle of the Inuit. Although many may view it as a negative shift and part of colonialism, many Inuit are Christian to this day.

As time went on, settlers used more resources in unsustainable ways and started establishing villages further north. Many Inuit communities were relocated to more northern villages by the government, this forced them to adapt their traditional way of life to territories that were not natural for them to inhabit in the new way that was expected of them; of course, that didn't work.

No one was aware of how delicate the balance of Indigenous life was in the Arctic, nor did they appreciate that it had been finely tuned over the course of millennia. The effects of the loss of culture and lifestyle were more harmful to the outcomes of the Inuit than anyone would have guessed. The loss of culture and lifestyle was extremely traumatic for the Inuit, without the traditional methods of hunting and survival many foods and resources became scarce and many lived in poverty conditions. To further add to the trauma of this upheaval was the utterly traumatic effects of the "residential schools" which will be discussed in a chapter all on its own.

The Haida People of the Pacific Northwest

Traditionally, many distinct Nations occupied the Pacific Coast on the mainland and on the many small islands around it. Despite having different cultures and languages, these Indigenous Nations shared at least one powerful resource in common: the ocean. The ocean defined the way of life for the traditional occupants of these beautiful territories. The People of the coast were well adapted to traveling over water and harvesting the abundant marine life that the Pacific Ocean had to offer.

The climate along the coast was drastically milder than the far north or even than other inland territories at the same latitudes. The Indigenous Peoples along the coast benefited from more forgiving temperatures and weather. They also benefited from the long growing season with ample diversity of flora and fauna in their territories. Finding food for survival was rarely an issue for the Indigenous Peoples of the Pacific Northwest.

The Haida Tribe
The Haida People lived on The Haida Gwaii archipelago, a

grouping of islands off the northwest coast of present-day British Columbia. There is evidence that the Haida have occupied that area for over 19,000 years. The entire area is thought to have been inhabitable even during the Ice Age-era as it would have been the southeastern part of Beringia. Based on traditional stories of the People living alongside the glaciers and western scientific methods, it is believed that the Haida people lived in the same territory during the Ice Age. When the Haida would have made their home in that area, the sea level was much lower, and the water that now separates the islands from the mainland would have been shallow and easily passable on foot throughout most of the year. The Haida had occupied their territory since a time when the rest of the world was covered with unfathomably massive glaciers.

After the Ice Age, the landscape began to change as the water levels gradually rose. The Haida people naturally adapted to a mariner lifestyle. They used the giant red cedars in their territory for many purposes, including dugout canoes of various sizes and uses. The Haida could travel quickly from island to island or the mainland with the canoes.

Food sources were plentiful on the Pacific Coast and offered the Haida People a diverse and nutritious diet. Their traditional diet included many fish and marine animals such as seals and whales. The Haida territory was also fortunate to have beavers, deer, bears, wolves, foxes, elk, and moose in their native environment. The people hunted whenever possible for food, pelts, and other parts. Unlike their Inuk neighbors in the north, the Haida and other coastal peoples also had access to abundant plants throughout the seasons, including fresh leafy greens and delicious berries.

The Haida had a unique culture, including a seemingly complex social structure based on hierarchy groupings, including enslaving people from conflicts with mainland tribes; other tribes knew them to be warriors, with a culture not unlike the Vikings.

The social structure of the Haida people was composed of two caste-like groups or moieties. The moieties were called the Raven Clan and the Eagle Clan. Each group held access to clan territories for hunting, fishing, or other resources that only clan members had the right to use. The moieties were made up of several closely related family group households of 30 or more people. Traditionally, the Haida was a matrilineal-based society, so the mother's relations determine the clan membership. There were many family groups in each clan, and every family had a male hereditary chief. Still, his heredity of the chiefdom was determined through matrilineal descent. The passing chief's eldest sister's son would be in line to be chief. Each household lived in their own large home with allotted land but alongside the other families of the same moiety.

Each clan was distinct and had its own traditional stories, songs, dances, and carving designs that the elders taught to the younger generations. Each generation took great pride in learning and maintaining the knowledge, cultural practices, and history.

Traditionally, when marriages took place, they were strictly between members of opposite clans to maintain diplomacy and diversity. The group that a child was a part of was determined matrilineally, meaning that they were members of the same group that their mothers were from, either Eagle or Raven.

In the traditional Haida culture, chores and duties were divided into gender roles for the most part. The Haida men were responsible for hunting, fishing, crafting canoes, homes, totems, and war-related activities. In the Haida culture, women were responsible for maintaining the living space—inside and out—and foraging for fruits and plants, caring for children, making clothing, and preparing food.

The unique and intricate traditional Haida culture is renowned for many things, but perhaps most notably for their artwork and craftsman skills. The Haida men were known as expert carvers, a skill that continues to be passed down today. They were known for carving giant canoes out of a single red cedar trunk. Some of the canoes were so large they could hold 50 people. The canoes were decorated with ornate carvings of animals that represented spirits and myths.

The Haida are perhaps most well-known for carving totem poles from giant red cedars. Other Indigenous Nations along the Pacific Coast also carved totem poles. The totems could range in size depending on the tree it was carved from; some were up to 70 feet in height. The style of the carvings on the totems was unique to the Haida and to the other coastal Indigenous Peoples who carved them. Totem poles were carved for many reasons, including to signify clan membership or show family lineage and honor certain myths, animals, people or events.

For most of the post-colonial era, European settlers believed that Indigenous culture was inherently evil and actively tried to eliminate it. From the late 1800s until the first few decades of the 1900s, European settlers banned, removed, and destroyed totems and other culturally significant Indigenous crafts and ceremonies. However, totems are now a famous and iconic symbol of Indigenous art and culture. Many people of all backgrounds travel to Haida Gwaii and other west coast destinations to view some of the oldest and tallest totem poles that remain in their original locations.

The large houses that the Haida families lived in were also built from the same red cedar as the canoes and totem poles, which were plentiful in the territory. The homes were large square-shaped structures that were windowless, though they did have venting in the ceiling to release the smoke from the fires that were used for heating and cooking. Each of the large buildings was home to one household of 30 or more people, including several nuclear families that were now-grown siblings who had spouses and children, other non-married family members, and elders. As previously mentioned, each of these households had a hereditary chief and preserved their history through stories, myths, songs, and carvings.

One of the main ceremonies that Haida practiced was the Potlatch ceremony. Potlatches were held for many reasons including to honor a passing or a birth. The ceremonies also served as a social event and could even be political in nature. Potlatches were used to demonstrate to others how wealthy and powerful a family was; all the hosts' valuable possessions including even enslaved laborers would be on display to prove their status in the community. The chief of the family hosting the Potlatch would offer gifts to all who came, including art, tools, boats, food, enslaved laborers, or territory rights for hunting and fishing. The ceremonies included ornate costumes, songs, and dance. The guests would be expected to remember and recount this generosity and wealth to continue to build up the host family's reputation of high social status and history. Negotiations between households or tribes could take place at Potlatches as well.

Haida spirituality was rooted in animal spirits and mythology based on Trickster spirits. They believed that animals were special, magical humans that could shape change into an animal or a human. It was believed that through reincarnation people's souls lived on in other physical forms, including animals. Each household had its own stories and beliefs about who had been reincarnated and on what farm, as well as stories about special animals that had been encountered.

A central figure of traditional Haida spirituality and mythology was the Raven Trickster. As a trickster spirit, the Raven was said to have the ability to go between the spiritual plane and the physical world. Raven was not considered to be a God but was the most powerful spirit in the Haida culture and spiritual beliefs. Raven was known as a benevolent trickster who enjoyed playfully confusing humans but did not cause harm unless provoked maliciously in some way.

There are many stories about Raven, called Wee'git in the Haida language, causing mischief and showing examples of why not to break rules, or playfully discovering misadventures because of his curiosity. There are many metaphors and themes that the Wee'git stories teach, including lightheartedness and curiosity.

In the Haida creation story, Wee'git uncovered the first Haida in a clamshell, here is a telling of the Haida Creation Story:

According to Haida legend, the Raven found himself alone one day on Rose Spit beach, on Haida Gwaii. Suddenly, he saw an extraordinary clamshell at his feet, and protruding from it were a number of small creatures. The Raven coaxed them to leave the shell to join him in his wonderful world. Some were hesitant at first, but eventually, overcome by curiosity, they emerged from the partly open clamshell to become the first Haida. (Raven Reads, 2018, para 12)

The Haida were proud warrior people with no fear of conflict or war. Traditionally the Haida warriors traveled by sea in huge carved cedar canoes which could hold up to 60 warriors. They traveled by sea to destinations both near and far, with stories recounting exploration and travel as far as California and Asia.

The warriors would paddle along the coast to trade with neighboring communities or simply to raid their adversaries' villages. During raids, the Haida would gain hunting or fishing territory, copper, and other precious resources. It symbolized power and prominence in Haida society to have many resources and keep enslaved laborers, whom the warriors acquired through raiding.

Traditional Haida warriors wore distinctive helmets ornately carved from cedar as well. For weapons, they used bows and arrows, spears, blowguns, clubs, daggers, and later firearms that they could carry in the canoes with them. They had shields to defend themselves from arrows and attacks as they approached the villages by the sea.

The Haida were formidable military strategists and expertly fortified their Island territory with towers, look-outs, and traps. Due to the geography of their homeland and their keen defense systems, they were virtually untouchable. From the towers, they could monitor the sea and beaches for any unwanted approaching boats and form an attack on them before they even landed on the shore. When European explorers began making contact along the west coast, they often documented the impressive and intimidating Haida warriors.

The Haida and Colonization

It wasn't until the 1770s that Europeans made their way to the pacific northwest and into the Haida territory. By all European accounts from the time of contact, they were impressed by the Haida Nation. The Europeans document an admiration for the Haida's defense system and the military's formidable seafaring abilities.

At the time of Haida's contact with the European explorers, the Haida had never seen or heard of non-Indigenous people. In contrast, the explorers had already encountered and probably interacted with a fair number of Indigenous Peoples on their travels. This left the Haida at a disadvantage. They mistook the pale European explorers as spirit people with different means and technology from their own. The Haida welcomed the newcomers because they believed that they were ancestral spirits of some kind.

At that time, the fur trade was a significant economic driver for the Europeans, and they soon began trading goods with the Haida in exchange for furs, which then were traded to merchants in China. As contact and trade increased relatively quickly on the west coast, compared to the east, the Haida soon replaced their traditional weapons for firearms that they traded for pelts.

As was the fate of all Indigenous Nations post-contact, the Haida contracted many illnesses from the European traders, including deadly smallpox and tuberculosis. It is estimated that these diseases were responsible for killing 95% of the Haida population; from such a great loss, the Nation never recovered. Today census data confirms that 501 people identify themselves as being of Haida descent, with 445 people still being able to speak the Haida language (Dorothy-Kennedy & Bouchard, 2010).

Despite a peaceful beginning to the relationship between the Haida and the European traders, tensions eventually mounted as more permanent European settlements were established in the area surrounding Haida Gwaii. The settlers and their emerging government believed that Indigenous traditions and customs were evil and the root cause of conflict between the two cultures. During the late 1800s, the settlers started to assert dominance and control over the Haida people and all Indigenous Nations in the pacific northwest. They enacted laws to eliminate Indigenous culture by banning traditional practices such as Potlatches and Totem Poles.

Throughout the 1900s, as the Haida population, culture, and traditional way of life had significantly declined, the settler government continued the campaign to further assimilate Indigenous Peoples by forcing Indigenous children from all parts of the continent into what are euphemistically called "residential schools." Today, most people referring to this practice refuse to call the institutions schools because they functioned more like forced detention facilities for children and youth; for that reason, in this book, that term is within quotations.

The outcomes of "residential schools" were devastating for the Haida, as it was for all Indigenous peoples. Children were forcibly and traumatically removed from their families and relocated to the "residential schools." The trauma affected parents and children alike and led to a disruption in appropriate cultural and family-based learning. Essential aspects of parental attachment were lost, not to mention that parenting skills are actually learned through modeling in a family setting; the disruption of that process resulted in a lack of continuity of socio-generational learning in a family environment; essentially, most Indigenous children during that era were not given the opportunity to be loved and parented, nor were they then able to learn how to be a parent.

The practice of removing children from their families went on for several generations. The trauma and effects were compounded with each generation until all that remained was a frail shell of a formerly glorious Nation. The language, culture, and joy were all but extinguished through these horrific colonial practices.

"Residential schools" have not been in operation for the past few decades, and though most of them closed before then, the effects remain today. In fact, very recently, thousands of stolen Indigenous children's remains have been discovered on the grounds of many former "residential schools." It is expected that as more former "residential school" sites are excavated that more missing children's remains will be uncovered. For Indigenous people, these findings are retraumatizing, but the discovery of the missing children's remains does allow for them to be returned to their families and communities. There is hope that this can at least bring some sense of closure and that a healing process may begin. It may also be true that the discovery of the gravesites brings further awareness to the true cruelty that took place in "residential schools"; a truth that was always known by Indigenous survivors and families, but that had been diminished or denied by governments over the past century.

The Nehiyawak (Cree) Nation in the Plains

Cree is the Anglicized name of the Nehiyawak Peoples, dubbed Cree due to miscommunication early on in their relationship with European trappers and settlers in the northeast. Traditionally the Nehiyawak Peoples' territory stretched across nearly the entire span of present-day Canada, from east of the Great Lakes, across the plains, to the foothills of the Rocky Mountains. The traditional lifestyle of the Nehiyawak was completely nomadic and involved following game across the great northern plains and sub-arctic boreal forests of the continent, which is why the Traditional Nehiyawak territory is so vast.

The Nehiyawak lived in relatively small family groups called a lodge. The members of each lodge would share daily living and labor tasks and would usually reside together in one tipi. Many lodges are grouped to form a community called a band. The band would collectively migrate to meet the seasonal needs together for most of the year.

Tipis were the main style of structure used by the nomadic Nehiyawak bands for shelter in all seasons. They are cone-shaped tents that the Nehiyawak people made from shaped wooden poles and buffalo, or sometimes other animal hides sewn together. There is evidence that Indigenous Peoples in the northern plains have been using tipis for over 5,000 years and even longer in the far north regions. This was the most common dwelling style for the Nehiyawak until the late 1800s when European settlers and government treaties forced Indigenous communities to stop living the traditional way and moved onto reservation land. Nowadays, tipis are generally only used for ceremonies and special events.

It was no coincidence that the tipi was the sheltering method of choice for nomadic bands since they were easy to erect and dismantle and relatively light to transport. Tipis were quite large; typically, they were anywhere between 12 and 20 feet wide at the base and stood 15 to 20 feet tall. Each tipi housed about 10 people, the average size of a lodge. An essential feature of the tipi was the hole in the very top point of the cone, which was necessary for venting the smoke from the fire that was used for cooking and heating.

For each season, the Nehiyawak had a different form of transportation to suit the climate and environment they would navigate. In the summer months, they would often use canoes to travel and transport their shelters swiftly and efficiently on water. Like everything that Indigenous Nations built and used, traditionally, canoes were made from what was available locally in their territories and for the needs of the people. Because of the different environmental requirements and readily available materials, the Nehiyawak and other inland Nations' canoes varied greatly from the Haida and west coast style canoes. The Nehiyawak made small, light canoes of birch bark; they created a spiny frame out of flexible branches and covered it with sewn birchbark flaps. These canoes were usually designed to hold only a few people with their gear and were more maneuverable than the large, heavy seafaring canoes that the Haida built.

In winter, the Nehiyawak people used sleds and snowshoes to traverse the deep snow. Like the canoes, sled frames were also made of birch wood. Animal hides were used to cover the frame and make a seat or platform for carrying gear. The sleds were different sizes depending on their use. Some sleds were pulled by dogs or horses while people simply pulled or pushed others. Traditionally, the Nehiyawak people used sleds to carry young children and belongings when migrating, or for hunting to carry supplies and to transport the animal.

Snowshoes are racquet-like woven platforms that were traditionally worn under moccasins and used to walk on top of the snow in winter, instead of sinking into the deep snow. They were traditionally made of birch wood and animal hide, bound tightly with a special rawhide weave to keep the structure.

The Nehiyawak used domesticated dogs and horses to help carry their belongings on a sled-like travois. A travois consisted of two birch wood poles joined together at a point on top to form a roughly triangular shape that was open at the bottom. Similar to a sled, objects of all sorts could be fastened to the travois and dragged along by the animal.

Traditional game hunted by the Nehiyawak would depend on the time of year and the territory that each group was familiar with or occupied. Often the Nehiyawak hunted and trapped large games such as deer, moose, elk, and caribou, and smaller games like rabbit, duck, turkey, and other birds or rodents that they could catch. Like all Indigenous peoples, the Nehiyawak lived sustainably; they hunted only as much as necessary and used every part of the animals they harvested.

Buffalo, which was plentiful in the prairies until 150 years ago, was a staple for the Paskwāwiyiniwak, the Plains Cree. The Paskwāwiyiniwak relied on the buffalo for food, hides, and trade with other bands and Nations. The giant animal could provide enough food for many people, and the thick hides had many traditional uses in the Nehiyawak culture. The Paskwāwiyiniwak used many techniques for hunting large animals, including bow and arrow, spears, and most efficiently, running them over a cliff's edge. In the plains, few locations worked as buffalo jump sites. Head-Smashed-In, located in southern Alberta (just north of the Canadian border from North Dakota), is a famous traditional site where the Paskwāwiyiniwak would run the buffalo over the cliffs. Buffalo bones collected at the cliff's foot were dated 6,000 years old. The Head-Smashed-In buffalo jump cliffs are a protected UNESCO World Heritage site to preserve the area and teach visitors to the park about Nehiyawak history.

Clothing was traditionally made by women in the Nehiyawak culture. Women would tan animal hides, especially deer, moose, and elk, to make leather for clothing and footwear. The women would then sew the clothing using needles made from animal bones and decorated with beadwork.

The Nehiyawak women mostly wore dresses made of leather with fringe and beadwork. The men wore coats with fringe cuts along the sleeves and decorative beadwork. The men's pants included underpants, similar to leggings or long johns, with leather chap-like panels called breechcloths over top. The pants were also decorated with beadwork and cut fringe. Typically, the clothing used in ceremonies and gatherings was more decorated with quills, furs, feathers, and ornate beadwork.

Moccasins are the handmade style of shoes that the Nehiyawak wore. Like the rest of the clothing, they were handmade by the women out of tanned hide and decorated the beadwork. Some moccasins were lined with fur on the inside to be extra warm or made into a taller boot style. Moccasins are still a popular and enduring Indigenous craft.

Intricate and ornate beading has been used in Indigenous peoples, including the Nehiyawak, to decorate clothing for at least 8,000 years. Each Nation, band, or even family has its own unique patterns and styles which are representative of the place, culture, and time the beader was working in. Traditionally beads were made of seeds, pieces of bones, small rocks, shells, and quills. The older styles of beading that have been discovered were larger and strung together like a necklace, rather than sewn directly onto the garment.

Traditional Nehiyawak Spirituality and Ceremonies

The most sacred ceremony in Nehiyawak culture was the Sun Dance. Each summer many bands of Indigenous Nations would gather for several days to dance and celebrate the gifts of life together. Depending on the size of the group gathered, they erected one or several lodges together to be used for the duration of the ceremony as shelter, kitchen, and for sweating.

A sweat lodge was also constructed for the sweat ceremony that was held at the beginning of the Sun Dance.

The Sun Dance ceremony was an important cultural tradition for Indigenous Peoples of the great plains and surrounding areas. It was the main time for people from different bands or even nations to come together to share songs, dance, and mythology in a ceremonial way. The experience of collectivity and sharing on a large scale solidified the values and culture each year; it also wove a common social and cultural thread to all the bands and nations who came.

Traditionally, the Sun Dance would last several days around the time of the summer solstice. This was a time to pray for healing and rebirth, sacrifices might be made for the good of the band or for an individual or family in need. The continuous dance and song of the ceremony were very intense for the dancers who would be dancing continuously in shifts for many days. This was the purpose of the ceremony, to sacrifice and continue the ceremony and practice despite the discomfort, to persevere and push past the personal obstacles as a sacred offering but also as an opportunity to discover one's own strength and capability. Some participants also performed other rituals based on the idea of creating a painful or challenging experience to overcome, for example, enduring skin piercing and pulling. The goal was to create a need to sacrifice personal comfort and to endure or overcome the sensation or physical needs that presented themselves through that experience.

The Sun Dance was also a time to check-in and learn from other bands and nations about things they had seen or heard over the years. Language and dialect varied between the bands and nations that came together during the Sun Dance.

Generally, neighboring bands would have a more similar dialect than ones who lived further apart. Despite the dialect differences, Nehiyawak could understand each other, although sometimes it might have taken a bit of effort.

Bands could pass on the news to each other at the Sun Dance; for example, people could share information about the happenings in other parts of the vast territory such as floods or fires, births and passings, and so on. Or, as the European explorers and trappers appeared in some areas of the Nehiyawak territory, that was passed on through social networks, including at the Sun Dance and through the relationships developed there.

A sweat lodge ceremony was performed as a part of the Sun Dance gathering and, at other times as a distinct ceremony on its own. Sweat lodge ceremonies are still practiced by many of the Nehiyawak bands today. In the center of a sweat lodge is a fire pit, the participants of the sweat sit in a ring around the pit and depending on the size of the group may form several rings. Once all the guests are in the lodge, the fire tender brings in rocks and adds them to the pit in specific placements. At this point, the entrance was closed, and the ceremony began with prayer. Sometimes the host would guide a prayer or participants of the sweat would pray in whatever way was meaningful to them. At times, the fire tender would also pour water onto the rocks to create steam and increase the heat. The sweat could last for nearly 24 hours with breaks taken by participants to avoid dangerous overheating.

The vision quest is another integral aspect of Nehiyawak spirituality. Vision quests were primarily performed by boys or youth transitioning into adulthood. It took quite a bit of time and dedication for the youth and the elders to make sure that the vision quester was prepared and ready for the experience. For youth in the Nehiyawak culture, it was a rite of passage to complete a vision quest, it showed that he was mature and was able to survive on his own in the wild.

Vision quests taught youth many valuable skills, both practical, cultural, and spiritual. They learned about the value of working toward something and achieving the privilege and opportunity to partake in this sacred ceremony. The vision quest was a goal and a reason for them to put energy into learning essential survival skills and cultural knowledge.

During the vision quest, the participant would spend several days on his own in the wilderness. The quest combined a practical time for youth to use survival skills as well as for them to experience an altered state of awareness and spiritual awakening.

It was believed that in order to achieve this altered state of consciousness and enter the spiritual realm, the youth should endure survival on their own with limited food and sleep. This also brought the participant into deep communion with his own thoughts, feelings, and experiences. The outcomes and visions were different for everyone. The visions that came had a unique meaning for each person. The participant gained new spiritual knowledge and understanding that was completely personal. In many Indigenous cultures, the vision and experience were kept secret and private for the participant.

Tobacco was also considered a sacred medicine in many Indigenous cultures, it was used in several ceremonies, including the profoundly sacred pipe ceremony. It represents the connection between the earthly world and the spirit world. The plant itself has deep roots which grow in the earthly physical world, yet, once it is dried and burned, it becomes smoke, which moves it from the physical world into the spiritual realm. It is a powerful metaphor for all things that exist in the physical world and their impermanence and ability to be transformed into an ethereal matter that disperses into the spirit world.

Sharing the smoke from tobacco also connects the people and their spirits as it passes from one to the next, and into the body then out into the world to be dispersed and to circulate infinitely; in that way, the tobacco smoke is connecting and unifying. Sharing the smoke from tobacco in the ceremony represents the desire to connect and share peace among people and spirits.

Traditionally, the Nehiyawak used the sacred plant tobacco in many ways, including as medicine. As healing medicine, tobacco smoke was blown by a medicine man onto wounds or onto a person in need of healing. It was also used as an offering, for example, by laying tobacco in a field with a prayer for a good harvest. It could also be used for other types of prayers and offered to an elder, family member, spirits and ancestors, and the creator, Gitchi Manitou.

Gitchi Manitou is the Great Spirit, also known as the Creator of the world. 'Gitchi' means great and 'Manitou' means spirit, making Gitchi Manitou the Great Spirit. The Great Spirit is a formless and genderless entity, not associated with being human. It was Gitchi Manitou who created the Earth, the plants, animals, and the people.

In the story of creation, Gitchi Manitou first created the four sacred elements: rock, water, fire, and wind. From those elements, Gitchi Manitou then created the earth, sun, moon, and stars. After the physical world was made, Gitchi Manitou created four types of plants: trees, vegetables, grasses, and flowers. Next Gitchi Manitou created four types of animals: four-legged, two-legged, flying animals, and swimming animals. After everything else was created, Gitchi Manitou made humans. Humans were considered to be the weakest of all of the creatures but had the unique power to think and dream.

The sacred mythology of the Nehiyawak, like that of all Indigenous Peoples, centered around animal spirits. This reflected the deep connection to nature and animals that Indigenous Peoples had. Traditionally, they believed in reincarnation so that animals might have spirits of people and vice versa. The interconnectedness of the people with the animals and nature was also reflected in spirituality and the respect for the delicate balance of life. The Nehiyawak understood the consequences of when life got out of balance and did what was within their power to maintain the balance through the way of life and also through prayer and ceremony.

The Nehiyawak also believed in animal tricksters. Wisakedjak is a trickster spirit of great import to the Nehiyawak culture and heritage. There are countless stories about Wisakedjak, a friendly but mischievous character who broke rules and caused the natural order of things to be upset and altered. Each band or community would have their own Wisakedjak stories to tell and to pass onto the younger generation to be kept and passed on for generations to come. The Nehiyawak trickster stories varied between bands and across their vast territory.

Here is a Nehiyawak story of why Gitchi Manitou created the trickster Wisakedjak borrowed from explorer David Thompson:

At the beginning of time, the Creator made the animals and the people. The Creator told Wisakedjak (a trickster figure) to teach the people how to live good, peaceful lives, and to take care of them. Wisakedjak did not listen to the Creator, and soon, the people were fighting and hurting one another. The Creator was disappointed and threatened Wisakedjak with a life of misery if he did not obey. Still, Wisakedjak did not listen, and still, the people continued to be violent with one another. The Creator decided to flood the lands, washing out everyone and everything. Only Wisakedjak, Otter, Beaver, and Muskrat survived. Stranded on open water, Wisakedjak had an idea — if the animals could help him dive down and collect some of the old earth, he could expand it and start a new land. This was not an easy task; Otter and Beaver tried many times to get to the earth below, but both failed, almost dying in the process. Muskrat was the last to try. He stayed underwater for a long time, but when he resurfaced, he had wet earth in his paw. From this mud is where the earth as we know it today came. (Preston, 2018, Origin Story)

Spirituality was a big part of traditional Nehiyawak wellness and medicine. The Medicine Wheel represents the Nehiyawak views of medicine and the holistic nature of wellness that was understood. In Nehiyawak culture, if someone was ill their entire life and circumstances would be evaluated in an attempt to understand the cause. According to traditional Indigenous medicine, illness could be caused by issues within one of four parts of a being. The Medicine Wheel was created as the traditional model of wellness among many Indigenous Nations. Causes of illness were considered to be more than just physical, for example, emotional or spiritual issues could be a cause.

The Medicine Wheel has four equal parts which make up the whole circle, the four parts correspond to the four directions: north, east, south, and west. Typically, the north is associated with the color white, east with yellow, south with red, and west with black or sometimes dark blue. Each part of the wheel is representative of an aspect of health, and together they create a holistic view of a person and their health. The north is the spiritual side of a person, the east is physical, the south is mental, and the west is emotional.

When a person is viewed as a whole and within the context of their environment, community, and circumstances, the causes and remedies of illness are understood differently than in the western world, where only the physical aspects are considered. In the traditional Indigenous view of wellness, someone with a seemingly physically-based wound or illness would be evaluated or considered in the context of their emotional, spiritual, and mental well-being. For example, if the ill person is mourning loss-making emotions and spirituality out of balance, that could be a reason for the illness; it would also inform the methods of treatment. To heal the spiritual wounds, the person might need to attend a sweat, a pipe ceremony, or a drumming circle. This helps the person integrate with their spirituality and allows healing to begin.

The holistic view of health as encompassing more than just the physical symptom of a disease is profound. The idea that spirituality and emotions are an integral part of overall health is slowly becoming more accepted in western medicine. It is now known to western doctors and health practitioners that mental health plays a big role in the overall well-being of a patient. The Indigenous holistic views of health have always attended to that reality. Interesting how that ancient knowledge and awareness was more sustainable and accurate than the western views that have attempted to replace it over the past 200 years.

Nehiyawak and the Effects of Colonialism

Nehiyawak people first encountered Europeans in the late 1600s in the vast and densely forested wilderness that is now called the Hudson Bay. Trappers and missionaries who had encountered other Indigenous Nations on the east coast were traveling westward to explore the rest of the continent when the Nehiyawak first made contact with them.

The relationship began, as most Indigenous-European ones did, with the Nehiyawak Nation welcoming the Europeans into their territory. Nehiyawak bands began to trade with European explorers and trappers to help them learn the way of the land, which most Europeans at the time were not familiar with.

As the demand for fur in Europe continued during the late 1600s and into the 1700s, the fur trade grew, and the interactions and relationships between Nehiyawak bands and the fur traders increased. The fur traders began establishing more permanent settlements in the Nehiyawak territory, including in the Hudson Bay area and beyond.

Some bands felt that they benefited from the fur trade with Europeans and were motivated to migrate or stay in that area to continue to trade, and many of them eventually chose to integrate more with the settlers. Because the Nehiyawak had always been a migratory and band-based nation—with networks and marriages happening between bands and cultures for time immemorial—it was natural for them to be more open to cross-cultural learning and relationships.

Whereas other bands were not as comfortable with the fur trade or with the growing numbers of settlers in the area; many of these bands relocated westward into the prairies. The Nehiyawak who migrated west from the forest to the prairies had to adapt to the new environment, they quickly learned many new skills such as buffalo hunting and traveling on horseback.

Many of the European settlements had missions from various Christian orders that operated churches, schools, and health services. Many Indigenous people were open to this new type of spirituality, learning, and health care and voluntarily integrated into the settlements through the missions. By integrating cultures and communities, an entirely new and distinct culture was born; the new culture consisted of families with an Indigenous mother and a French settler father. As cross-cultural relationships became common, the families banded together to form a distinct culture called the Métis Nation.

Treaties became a critical factor in Indigenous and Euro-settler relations in the 1800s. At first, they were allegedly created in an effort to settle disputes and the question of land ownership and land use rights. Treaties significantly impacted the Indigenous way of life for the Nehiyawak people. It was particularly impactful to the traditional migration-based lifestyle to be confined to such a small space.

Many Indigenous communities, especially across the prairies, were coerced into signing the treaties as colonizers withheld supplies or other resources from them if they did not cooperate. Other bands and groups were promised future considerations or protections of their sovereignty if they signed treaty agreements.

Although the intended outcome of the treaties in the prairies was allegedly to limit interactions and conflicts between the Nehiyawak and other nations with Euro-settlers, they had the opposite effect. Around the same time that treaties were being signed, the colonial and settler governments were also making laws against traditional Indigenous cultural practices. The Canadian and American governments also created new policing systems at that time to keep Indigenous People on the reserve land and prevent the cultural practices that had been banned. This greatly affected the Nehiyawak with their traditional nomadic lifestyle.

Understandably, the treaties and laws only created more tension and conflict between Indigenous Nations and the settlers. Again, in a further misguided attempt to mitigate the conflicts, the government decided that Indigenous children should be assimilated into the Settler-Canadian culture by forced attendance in the "residential schools." Especially across the prairies, the government also enforced attendance at the schools through the newly created policing system, the Royal Canadian Mounted Police. Children were forcibly removed from their families and communities and brought to the "residential schools" against anyone's wishes and without consent. Tragically, as mentioned in the previous section, many children never returned home, and their families were never notified of what happened to them; most families were left to mourn and wonder what horrible fate had become their children forever. Those that did return were never to be the same. The amount of abuse and neglect they faced caused generational trauma that profoundly affects all Indigenous people.

Even though the "residential schools" are now closed and some other advancements for Indigenous rights have been made, there is still a lot of injustice and racism against Indigenous people in North America. Both systemic and overt racism continues to inhibit and affect Indigenous Peoples today, not to mention the lingering effects of the trauma that has impacted many generations. A lot of racism the Indigenous people are currently facing is systemic. Such things as the quantifiably poorer health outcomes for Indigenous people can be attributed in many ways to systemic racism; due to a lack of accessible health care resources, being dismissed and not heard or believed by healthcare professionals, and even from such seemingly basic barriers like a lack of potable water on reserves.

The Haudenosaunee (Iroquois) Confederacy in the Northeast

The Haudenosaunee Confederacy, more commonly known as the Iroquois Confederacy, is a coalition of six Indigenous groups who created a powerful league of peaceful and cooperative nations. It is unclear exactly when the five founding Nations established the confederacy, although oral Haudenosaunee history suggests that it may have existed in some form as early as the mid-1100s. However, that fact is disputed by western scientists who argue that the archaeological evidence dates back to the mid-1400s.

The Nations of the Haudenosaunee Confederacy occupied the Northeastern region of the United States, mostly, what would be considered New England in the present day, and north from there into Southern Canada. Initially, the Confederacy members were the Kanien'kehá:ka (Mohawk), OnΛyoteʔa·ká (Oneida), Onoñda'gega' (Onondaga), Gayogohó:nǫ' (Cayuga), Onödowa'ga:' (Seneca). Later, in 1722, the Skarù·rę? (Tuscarora) people joined. The confederacy was known to the European fur traders and settlers as the Six Nations.

It is said that the Confederacy was created as a peace agreement between five founding Indigenous Nations. The peace agreement called The Great Law of Peace was expressed as a principle by a visionary leader and medicine man, Deganawida, The Great Peacemaker. It's not clear exactly what his life was like or from which nation he originated. He met Hiawatha, a great and legendary leader from the Onondaga and Mohawk peoples. It's not an exaggeration to say that their meeting and relationship impacted the lives of millions of people throughout history. They discussed the philosophy of peace and laid out the principles of The Great Law of Peace. It is rare in history that two people so visionary and pure of the heart come together to make political decisions. They were true philosopher-kings who led with the genuine intention of bettering the social and political world of the Haudenosaunee Peoples.

The two men gathered leaders from five nations who were feuding for centuries to agree on peace. At that time, the nations worked together to create the Gayanashagowa (Great Law of Peace). It was customary for records to be kept in the form of beaded sash-like creations called wampum. That is how their history was held, through the oral tradition of passing on stories from one generation to the next, which were aided by the wampum.

The agreement that the Nations came to is similar to a modern-day constitution; it outlined members' expectations and responsibilities, the scopes of power of the leaders, and how leaders would be selected and removed. According to Alaka Wali, the constitution of the Haudenosaunee Confederacy included these tenets that are now well recognized as key features of successful democracies (Wali, A., 2016):

- A restriction on holding dual offices
- Processes to remove chiefs from the confederacy leadership
- A multi-level legislature with procedures in place for passing laws
- A method of how and when to declare war
- According to later transcriptions, the creation of a balance of power between the Iroquois Confederacy

and individual tribes.

The Grand Council of the Haudenosaunee Confederacy consisted of about 50 chief representatives; initially, there were 14 chiefs from the Onondaga, 10 from the Cayuga, nine chiefs each from the Oneida and the Mohawk Nations. When the Tuscarora joined, they were non-voting members. All decisions had to be made by a unanimous consensus, and when members brought matters to the Grand Council for lawmaking, each Nation had a role in considering the case. First, an issue would be considered by the Seneca and Mohawk chiefs, after which they would pass it on, along with their thoughts, to the Oneida and Cayuga Chiefs for further deliberation. Finally, the Onondaga Chiefs were the final decision-makers of the process. They would hear what the others had to say and ensure a unanimous consensus before turning any matter into law. This system was the most thorough way to ensure democracy was served and to avoid an imbalance of power in the hands of just one individual chief or nation.

Although this Confederacy was not the first or last, it is the most enduring. The Haudenosaunee Confederacy is now known to be the longest-running democratic system globally. Several factors appear to have set this confederacy apart from others; it was well defined and well organized with a complex electoral system that included checks and balances. These factors seem to have made the coalition generally more effective and, in turn, more enduring than any other.

Because each Nation was made up of several community groups, each group was then made up of several clans, ensuring that all people were adequately represented was complicated. The Confederacy uses a unique and complex electoral system based on the matrilineal principles typical of many Indigenous peoples, including those of the Haudenosaunee Confederacy.

The Haudenosaunee culture was matrilineal. Each family had a designated Clan Mother, who was traditionally the eldest female family member, although now she is generally chosen by consensus because of her devotion to the traditional culture and family. Each family lived in a communal longhouse, grouped through the women's relations. When people married, traditionally the man would move into his wife's family's longhouse and no matter where he lived, he would always retain his original membership to his mother's clan.

The Clan Mother of each family was responsible for selecting the clan chief called the Hoyaneh, who was always a man. The Clan Mother also had the power to remove Hoyaneh from their positions if she felt he was not properly representing the clan. Aside from selecting the Hoyaneh, the Clan Mother was responsible for naming the members of the clan, ensuring that everyone was cared for and well-fed, and making many decisions for the clan.

At the time that they joined forces, the Nations that made up the Confederacy were agriculturists and predominantly sedentary. They were relatively early adopters of farming practices and grew what is known as the three sister crops: corn, beans, and squash, which were the earliest and prominent subsistence crops grown by Indigenous Peoples in the Americas. Cultivating the three sisters offered many benefits to the Haudenosaunee Confederacy, including a relatively reliable food source that they could have a greater degree of control over. With the consistency of an agriculture-based society, came a more sedentary lifestyle, which revolved around the crops and the work to tend them.

The agricultural lifestyle was relatively relaxed for the Haudenosaunee people. The men cleared fields in early spring and the women and older children spent most of the spring and summer seeding and tending to the crops. Men would be busy with hunting and other seasonal tasks during those months, which included building and repairing houses.

After the transition to agriculture, the Haudenosaunee people built permanent shelters and started living in one place year-round. The houses they built were called longhouses, and the name Haudenausonee means the "People of the Longhouse." The switch to agriculture and sedentary living freed up time formerly spent migrating and repeatedly reestablishing shelters and camps. The Haudenosaunee lifestyle was relatively relaxed as a result, and the people were well cared for, including any enslaved laborers that the Haudenosaunee took during wars.

The transition to agriculture occurred before the confederacy of the Haudenosaunee Nations was formed. During the time before the coalition was established, nations fought over hunting and gathering territories and other issues that arose from occupying neighboring territories. They would often take war prisoners from each other to enslave as laborers as well as to adopt as replacements for dead relatives. As the formerly nomadic nations settled into permanent settlements, it became more desirable and efficient to have peace. It also helped to create more safety in a larger group if necessary.

Before the arrival of the Europeans, the traditional rivals of the Haudenosaunee were the Huron, the Mohicans, and at times other neighboring nations. The prime motive of war at that time was to take captives for enslaved labor and protect or take over hunting territory. Largely because of the demand for enslaved laborers, the Haudenosaunee did not glorify killing their rivals in battle. They also profoundly valued the lives of their own people and strove to minimize the loss of warriors as much as possible.

In the Haudenosaunee culture, grieving was a very important aspect of spirituality. Family and friends deeply mourned those who passed, especially in battle. There were many sacred rituals that attended to the grieving process and honored the dead. The first was the condolences ceremony, where attendees were divided into two groups, the first was the most directly affected who were mourning, and the second group was the relations who were less directly affected, and they were the comforting group. The nation of the deceased hosts the condolence ceremony unless there were special circumstances or reasons that they could not, in which case it would be hosted by another nation. The members of the other nations would come to visit and offer condolences and comfort to the nation of the deceased. If the deceased was a chief, then a replacement would often be chosen at the same time and appointed.

Another traditional grieving practice of the Haudenosaunee was the revenge-seeking mourning-wars. If a warrior or chief died in battle, it was customary for the clan and nation to seek revenge in the form of a mourning war. The mourning nation would raid and attack the rival village to kidnap hostages. Once the mourners took the hostages and brought them back to their own village, they tortured them ritualistically.

The torture was a communal practice that involved participation from everyone in the community, including children. Communal torture like this was not unique to the Haudenosaunee nations, in fact, it was typical for all

Indigenous Nations in the northeast woodlands during the time period. The length and severity of the torture reflected the mother's grief from the loss; if the loss was particularly painful and the mother was particularly bereaved, the torture would be more severe. It was a vengeful and cathartic practice.

After the torture, there were two outcomes that could become of the captive. The first, yet less common, the outcome was simply death. The second was a form of adoption into the mourning family, as a replacement for the member who was lost. The mourning mother would decide to either keep the captive as a member of her clan, to replace the one who was lost, or to kill the captive.

Generally, the captives were adopted as the Haudenosaunee didn't believe in unnecessary death. The traditional belief was that when a member was lost, the group lost some power and became weaker. For that reason, the clans adopted a replacement member. Once the replacement was brought into the family they generally stayed and became a member of the group.

Although war and torture were a part of the Haudenosaunee culture for a long time, through the confederacy the Gayanesshagowa, the Great Law of Peace, it was a major goal of the Haudenosaunee to try to find peace among themselves and with all other peoples. The Gayanesshagowa outlined many ways for conflicting nations to recognize the suffering of one another and to attempt to alleviate the loss of lives and resulting suffering.

One of the most sacred and renowned ceremonies associated with the Gayanashagowa is the Great Tree of Peace. When the confederacy was born, the nations planted a white pine and buried their weapons beneath it. This symbolized leaving war and weapons behind and growing a better, less violent, and traumatic future together. It became a symbol that was used with other nations as well, including with the Europeans when they began exploring the eastern part of the continent.

The Haudenosaunee and European Contact

When the Europeans arrived, the fur trade and the weapons that came with them created a shift in the dynamic that had been established between the Haudenosaunee and their neighboring tribes, the Huron and Algonquians. Alliances were formed between the various Indigenous Nations and the various European traders.

The Haudenosaunee were sought-after trading partners and allies for the recently landed Europeans. Their territory was well located on the eastern seaboard, and they controlled a large part of the land.

Perhaps the most notorious aspect of Haudenosaunee and European contact is the series of conflicts known as the French-Iroquois Wars or the Beaver Wars. These wars have gone down in history as some of the bloodiest wars in American history. It's hard to imagine that these wars were fought over beavers, for that matter, it's hard to believe that most of the conflict between the Indigenous Nations and the Europeans was for such frivolous and passing trends.

The first contact between the Haudenosaunee and the French occurred in 1609. Early relations were strained between the two peoples due to Samuel de Champlain killing three Haudenosaunee chiefs. This, of course, created a rivalry and adversarial relationship from the beginning. They continued to battle on and off until the 1700s.

At that time, the Dutch and the Haudenosaunee were the main trading partners in the fur trade. The Haudenosaunee controlled the largest territory on the Northeast coast with plenty of beaver habitat. They had the advantage of good supply and strong trade with the Dutch who were initially the largest purchasers of beaver pelts in the area.

What further strained the relationship between all groups in the Northeast, Indigenous and European was the rapid depletion of the beavers in the area. With the high demand of beaver pelts for trade and the introduction of European firearms to the Indigenous Nations of the Northeast, including the Haudenosaunee, the beaver population quickly declined. As beavers became less available, the Haudenosaunee sought to take more land in order to maintain control of the fur trade. They began to fight wars to expand their territory and ended up displacing other tribes who were forced to relocate further west.

Wars and conflicts continued as the European nations also fought each other for control of the fur trade, land use, and resources. As European settlements became more common and more permanent, especially along the eastern seaboard and the main river junctions inland, the settlers wanted more control over the territory. The Haudenosaunee Confederacy became the main representation of the tribes in the Northeast, including the six-member tribes, but they also included and negotiated on behalf of several more tribes. The strong and well-established confederacy was a great benefit to all Indigenous Nations in the area as it united and amplified the voices that only gained power from being aggregated and otherwise would have been completely defeated and dominated by the European forces and settlers.

After nearly a century of conflict in the Northeast, a peace agreement was made between the Haudenosaunee, the French, and the English. The French occupied the area to the

North of the Haudenosaunee territory, and the English occupied the South. The Haudenosaunee territory created a buffer zone between the two rivals, and they were able to trade and create relationships with both colonies.

The peaceful period did not last long and by the early 1700s, the Haudenosaunee population had declined considerably due to war and to the newly introduced European diseases. With the peace in the area, European colonies were growing quickly, and they were soon trying to push their territory boundaries into the Haudenosaunee land, which created a new spark in conflict.

In the mid-1700s the French and Indian War was fought. It was a multifaceted battle that had several warring sides. The Haudenosaunee sided with the British who had been their allies for many decades at that point and with whom they had a functional if not beneficial relationship. The other warring parties included the French to the North, who were backed by the Algonquian Nation. Following this war, the British continued to reward the Haudenosaunee by signing land treaties for use as Confederacy reserve land and would be protected and held under their control. The amount of land that was lawfully and practically Haudenosaunee territory during the 1700s was sizable. However, over the following decades, the Haudenosaunee gradually ceded large quantities back to the British.

The next conflict that disrupted the peace for the Haudenosaunee and the entire "New World" was the American Revolution. The Haudenosaunee attempted to remain neutral in the conflict between the settled Americans and the British Empire. To the Haudenosaunee, the two groups were not distinct, and they failed to fully understand what the conflict was about. They viewed all the English speakers as one united group. They also didn't want to choose a side because they had a good working relationship with both the British and the Americans. Eventually, due to their long history of trade and allyship, the Confederacy was pressured to support the British.

This war is ultimately what ended up disbanding the Confederacy as not all the Nation members were supportive of the British. Each Nation of the Confederacy ended up going their own way at this point and the Alliance ended. The American Revolution affected the nations of the Haudenosaunee greatly, leaving them with many more casualties and villages destroyed by war. After the war ended, the lifestyle and quality of life for Indigenous Nations began to decline more steadily.

The general tension between Indigenous peoples and settlers increased as the sense of domination and oppression increased. There were more treaties being signed and they were being more strictly enforced. After the Revolution, the new governments of Canada and the United States started to create more laws to prohibit the practice and expression of Indigenous culture and traditions. The former members of the Haudenosaunee Confederacy, like all Indigenous people in the US and Canada, were also subjected to forceful and unconsented removal of children who were then placed in "residential schools" where many perished or disappeared.

Although the treaties stated that Indigenous People, especially those whose traditional territory straddled the American-Canadian border, had the right to travel between the two countries and purchase or bring goods across without paying duties; it took a long time and a lot of activism for these rights to be recognized. Over time more rights have been recognized but it was not without a fight, and not without grave harm and trauma caused by the discrimination and oppression. Such is the way with most aspects of rights and freedoms for Indigenous people in the Americas, and indeed across the globe.

The Choctaw Nation in the Southeast

The Choctaw Nation traditionally inhabited a large territory in the Southeastern United States, where it is now Oklahoma, Alabama, Mississippi, and Louisiana. The Choctaw language, Chohta, is considered a part of the Western Muskogean Languages and is the native language of nearly 10,000 people living in the United States. There are several tribes that make up the Choctaw Nation and each has its own distinct stories and history. As with all Indigenous Nations included in this book, this is a generalized account of the history, as each specific Nation, tribe, clan, family, and even individual would have their own accounts of what life was.

The Choctaw are descended from the Mound Building peoples who populated what is now southeastern North America for over 5,000 years. Archaeological evidence places the Mound Builders at several sites, the Choctaw descended from the Mississippian Mound Builders, which was the third and final era or stage of the Mound Building Culture. Mound Building cultures had developed hierarchical social structures with an elite or ruling class and a subordinate or laboring class. This represented a certain level of sophistication and complexity in social organization that would have evolved in a stable group over a long time. It indicates a long history as a people that organized in complex ways over time. This type of social structure can only happen as population size increases due to the agrarian and sedentary lifestyle.

The Mound Builder cultures used the labor of the lower-class members to create impressive earthen mound structures. The mounds generally had four sides and were leveled on the top to be a platform, like a flat-topped pyramid constructed with compressed dirt. The laborers who built the mounds would excavate the dirt from one site and transport it in baskets to the mound site, they would then dump the dirt onto the mound and trample it down by foot. Eventually, the mounds would take shape into a large, often tiered platform structure. Sometimes more tiers would be added at later times from the original construction.

Although they had various purposes, each mound was sacred; some were used as a burial site for chiefs or other important members of the group, others were extravagant platforms for the chief's dwelling, others were used as political places where groups would gather to discuss trade and other diplomatic issues.

Like many Indigenous Nations, the Choctaw Nation was divided into two groups or moieties. Each moiety consisted of three districts and each district had several clans with each clan consisting of several groups who occupied their own towns and villages. The Choctaw society was complex and well organized with many levels of leadership and governance. The chiefs of the districts were called mingos and were chosen for having strong characteristics and leadership abilities which included a history of military achievement, good ancestry, good organization, and ability to communicate well. This system ensured that the Choctaws were governed in a democratic way and that all people were adequately considered and represented.

Marriages were only allowed to happen between moieties. Following the matrilineal tradition, children were considered a part of the moiety and clan from which their mother originated.

The Choctaw were an agrarian and sedentary people from a relatively early point in the history of Indigenous Nations in the Americas, as evident from their descending from the Mississippian Mound Builders. They produced the staple three sisters' crops of corn, beans, and squash.

Like all Indigenous Peoples, the Choctaw's lifestyle was seasonal and revolved around what was necessary and possible to do in each distinct time of the year. Chores and tasks were also divided by gender roles and between classes in the hierarchical society.

Traditionally, the new year began at the spring equinox; at that time most of the people, regardless of gender and age, would participate in sowing the seeds for the sustenance crops. From that point on, it was mainly the women and children who tended to the crops, ensuring they were watered and weeded throughout the increasingly hot months of summer.

In spring, while the women and children were occupied in the fields, the men would go hunt and trap small game such as rabbits, wild hogs, turkeys, and any other available protein sources. The women would process the meat to be prepared for eating and the men would process and tan the hides, rendering them useful for making clothes, blankets, and other essentials.

Over the summer, tending the crops continued to be the main priority and kept most of the women and children busy. When the crops were ripened at the end of summer it was time for a sacred celebration of life and the gifts of harvest. The celebrations included a deeply spiritual aspect, and the participants would pray and fast to focus on forgiveness and new beginnings. This was the main spiritual and cultural event of the year.

During the fall, hunting large game became the focus for the Choctaw men. They hunted deer, bears, and other large animals. The women would focus on processing the meat. A major celebration event occurred late in the fall, before winter when things became quieter, and people spent more time making crafts and telling stories.

The Choctaw women and men were skilled crafters who were renowned for their woven baskets made from river cane, pottery from river clay, shell jewelry and beads, as well as fine fabric made from mulberry bark. Winter was a good time for crafting as it provided a natural break from the field and agriculture-related labor.

Building houses and other necessary structures was another occupation that employed the labor of both women and men. The houses were permanent structures, traditionally constructed with heavy posts and beams made from locally and intentionally harvested lumber. The men were responsible for providing and setting the heavy posts and frame of the house. The women would then complete the structure by adding mud and grass in a specialized technique to fill in the walls. The roofs were made from thatched river grasses and later covered in tree bark as well.

Most men were also warriors and athletes who trained hard year-round to provide protection for the villages. The Choctaw people were known as peaceful people, raiding was not a part of their culture. However, they did maintain an active and well-trained warrior force that focused more on defensive tactics than raiding or attacking. As such, it was the philosophy that the warriors must be very skillful in order to appropriately defend women and children in their own territory and villages.

Ishtaboli, or stickball in English, which is a traditional Indigenous sport played by many Indigenous Nations, was a big part of the Choctaw culture as well. Ishtaboli was played using sticks with woven baskets on the end to catch and throw the ball, the ball must hit a goal post situated at either end of a long-playing field in order for the team to score. It is the origin sport of Lacrosse which is gaining popularity today.

Ishtaboli was played by the men in the Choctaw tribe, they put a lot of time and energy into training for the sport. Ishtaboli was very competitive with many nations competing against each other in big matches and tournaments which could include hundreds of players or more and have thousands of spectators. The game rules were relatively elaborate, players each portrayed and embodied an animal spirit in their costume and sporting style. Ishtaboli was also extremely physical, with many injuries and even deaths occurring as a result. The skills and athletics learned from playing Ishtaboli were used as a form of training for the warriors of the tribe.

Traditionally the Choctaw played many other games as pastimes and entertainment and not all were as physical as Ishtaboli. Other games included one that used painted seeds in a similar way to dice throwing and another where objects would be hidden in shells.

The Choctaw and European Contact

Because the Choctaw were situated near the Atlantic on the Southeast side of North America, they were one of the first Indigenous nations to have contact with the European explorers in the early 1500s. At this time, they were subjected to all of the diseases that plagued Indigenous People from the time the Europeans arrived and the population declined significantly.

It was the Spaniards who first encountered the Choctaw and took a mingo hostage. The Spaniards demanded that the Choctaw give them resources such as canoes, laborers, and women in exchange for the return of the chief. Tuscaloosa, the kidnapped mingo, escaped and refused to release the laborers and women. A battle ensued in which an entire Choctaw village was burned, and hundreds of Choctaw people were killed, as well as two dozen Spaniards.

It wasn't until the 1700s that the French began to establish permanent colonial settlements and trading posts in Choctaw territory along the Mississippi River. Due to their naturally peaceful nature and formally established villages and societal structure, the Choctaw were early allies and trading partners with the French, however, the impact of European contact remained relatively minor for the most part.

It wasn't until the 1800s when American contact gradually became more frequent and affected the Choctaw People. Due to encroaching American villages and treaties, the Choctaw eventually ceded most of their territory in Mississippi to the Americans in exchange for land and freedom in Oklahoma. The majority of Choctaw moved westward into Oklahoma, with some also settling in Texas at that time.

The Choctaw remained peaceful and open to interactions with Americans but even so, eventually, the Americans began to establish more and more so-called "anti-Indian" laws and practices to try to eliminate Indigenous culture and to "civilize" the people. Finally in the mid-1800s after several hundred years of relatively peaceful coexistence with the white man, the Choctaw fought back. The battle lasted two days and was not victorious for the Choctaw. Many Choctaw escaped to Mexico at that time or joined other tribes in

Oklahoma.

To this day the effects of the American "anti-Indian" sentiment can be felt and observed. As history and traditions were lost when the lineage of the oral tradition and practice was interrupted. Sadly, many of the Indigenous Nations in the southern United States were also subjected to the "residential schools" designed to civilize the Indigenous Peoples in America. The trauma of families being separated lasted for several generations and continues to affect the lives of hundreds of thousands of people today.

The Ben 'Zaa (Zapotec) People of Southwestern Mexico

The Ben 'Zaa is the name by which the Zapotec people now self-identify. Ben 'Zaa means the cloud people and they call themselves that because they believed that the clouds were the divine beings from which they were created and that upon death they would return to the clouds. The Ben 'Zaa is more commonly known as the Zapotec people and is made up of several groups who shared the Zapotec culture and civilization. They are a large Indigenous group who have occupied the Oaxaca region in southwestern Mexico for millennia, where they were dominant and well established from as early as 1100 B.C.E. The Indigenous language was called Zapotecan and included a written form that used glyphs from an early time in history.

The Zapotecs established complex permanent villages and cities, with the largest and most enduring being Monte Albán, which was known as the political center or capital of the Zapotec civilization. Monte Albán was heavily fortified, indicating that there was many conflicts and many battles in Zapotec history requiring the overall need for defense in the time and place that the city was built. The walls of the fortified city were adorned with many stone slabs with carved images depicting military victory and power, as well as the terrible outcomes for the war captives from rival groups. It was indeed an impressive and intimidating city that provoked both awe and submission.

Monte Albán was an elaborate city and shows the overall level of social organization and sophistication of the Zapotec people at the time. The city included elaborate architecture that was laid out with both intention and attention to detail in perfect north-south lines. The sophisticated urban design plans included dams and canals to provide access to water, gymnasiums for sports and games, religious temples and burial sites, elegant dwellings for the upper class, common dwellings alongside as well as open communal space. The stone buildings and walls of the city were all skillfully and elaborately carved, illustrating both the opulence and the appreciation of art in the Zapotec culture. The remains of Monte Albán are impressive, and the site is recognized as a UNESCO World Heritage site that draws visitors from all over the world.

If Monte Albán was the political and economic center of the ancient Ben 'Zaa civilization, then Mitlá was considered the religious capital. The name Mitlá is a Hispanicised variation of the word Mictlan, which means a resting place for the dead. The city was completely ornate, and it is clear and easy to observe how much work went into building it with every structure decorated with beautiful and elaborately patterned masonry. The city was believed to be the earthly gateway to the afterlife in the clouds and was used as the burial site for the Zapotec elite to ensure that they would be returned to the clouds.

For those Zapotecs who were not of the elite ruling class, it was believed that they originated in caves and were somehow descended from the jaguar and puma which both played central roles in mythology and religion. The common Zapotecs had different burial practices and ceremonies from the elite. Many were buried with their prized possessions beneath the floor of the family home so that they could return to the earth and still be able to communicate with their family, in this way the ancestors remained a sacred part of the Zapotec family.

Other traditional religious ceremonies included sacrificial offerings of animals and at times even humans. The sacrifices, which often included removing a beating heart, were made as offerings to the Gods in an attempt to influence and persuade them to improve conditions that were out of human control. Often the sacrifices were made to Cocijo who was the Zapotec god of storms and rain.

The Zapotec civilization was highly organized and specialized, much like society today, with people occupying many specific roles. There were elites who ruled and governed at various levels, then the majority of the population who filled functional roles in the society such as potters, theists, linguists and scribes, builders, masons and sculptors, jewelers who crafted fine pieces from gold, athletes, agricultural food producers, and so on.

The most popular Zapotec sport, as evidenced by the arenas built into the cities, was known as a ballgame. The location of the ballgame arenas in the central and religious areas of the cities indicates that the sport was a very important aspect of the Zapotec culture. The game was played in a similar way to soccer as it involved moving a ball between players by only using feet and scoring points by passing the ball through goalposts. The ball was much harder, and the sport may have been rougher between players than soccer is today. The Zapotec players wore more protective gear to avoid injuries from getting hit with the ball. There are many depictions of ballgames being played in Zapotec and Mayan art, including on ceramics and in stone carving. Some of the depictions of the matches end in a ceremonial sacrifice. There is still a version of this game played in the Oaxaca region of Mexico today.

Zapotecan was also a highly evolved language and included a written form that used glyphs to represent each syllable of a word. The glyphs were used to record history and keep records and are believed to be the oldest written language of Mesoamerica. The Zapotecs also developed and used a calendar system to track the passage of time according to cycles of the moon and seasons.

At the height of their power, the Zapotecs were actively expanding and dominating villages and cities beyond the Oaxaca territory, creating a massive empire that is estimated to have reached over 500,000 people. The effects of the expansion and domination can be observed in the archaeological records as styles of pottery and art-making suddenly changed as the Zapotecs overtook each village.

The Zapotecs and European Contact

Unfortunately for the Indigenous Peoples of Mesoamerica, it was the Spaniards who first explored the area with the intent to discover and colonize. The Spaniards had a less diplomatic approach to colonization than the French and English did in the same era. Whereas the French and English initially sought to trade with and learn from the Indigenous Peoples they encountered, the Spaniards were known as more ruthless colonizers; they killed as many Indigenous People as possible and tried to conquer and wipe out the cultures as much as possible.

Right around the time that the Europeans were first exploring the region now known as Mexico, the Zapotecs were engaged in a series of battles with the Aztecs. The Aztecs were becoming the dominant force between the two although they had yet to conquer the Zapotecs.

Shortly after the final battle between the Zapotecs and the Aztecs, the Spaniards arrived. They first encountered the Incas and Aztecs. Like the other European explorers and traders, The Spanish conquistadors spread diseases throughout the Indigenous villages, immediately lowering the populations and limiting their ability to adequately defend themselves. The Aztecs and Incas were the first of the Mesoamerican civilizations to be conquered by the Spaniards.

Having heard this news, the Zapotecs, hoping for a more diplomatic outcome, attempted to avoid the same fate by avoiding attacking the Spaniards. The tactic did not work and ultimately the diseases and the conquistadors decimated the Zapotecs as well. After the Spaniards conquered Mexico, very few Indigenous People remained alive and many of those who did survive were ill-fated to become enslaved by the Spanish colonies.

CHAPTER 6
CONTEMPORARY ISSUES OR TREATIES AND LAND USE

In the minds of most North Americans, particularly those who are descendants of settlers, colonialism is over. This is likely because the present-day nations that dominate, occupy, and govern the land and people of North America are so well established. For Indigenous People, however, colonialism continues, as their rights and sovereignty continue to be encroached upon.

Much of the conflict that remains between Indigenous Nations and settler governments stems from the cultural differences in the meaning of some of the agreements made. The fundamental differences in views meant that even though each nation believed that they were understanding each other and signing a treaty or agreement that had the same meaning for each party, the truth is, they weren't. The underlying beliefs about the meaning of the agreements were completely different without either party realizing the impact that would have on the way that the treaties were put into practice. The differing views are described in the Canadian Encyclopedia:

On the one hand, is the government's view of treaties as legal instruments that surrendered Indigenous rights. On the other is the Indigenous view of treaties as instruments of relationships between autonomous peoples who agree to share the lands and resources of Canada. Seen from the Indigenous perspective, treaties do not surrender rights; rather, they confirm Indigenous rights. Treaties recognize that Indigenous peoples have the capacity to self-govern. Bridging the gap between these two views of treaties poses a huge challenge to people and lawmakers in Canada. (Hall, 2017, para 7)

Due to the lack of cultural understanding between the Indigenous Nations and the settler governments, it seems that in the eyes of the settlers the Indigenous Nations had signed away more rights than they believed they had. Subsequently, when the governments began using more force to attempt to control and enforce the treaties and "anti-Indian laws," it created more conflict between the Indigenous Nations and the governments.

There is a major imbalance of power in the relationship between Indigenous Nations and contemporary colonial governments. This imbalance stems from many factors including the long history of racist attitudes and policies toward Indigenous Peoples and their cultures, as well as the relatively small population of Indigenous People and the dispersion of the Indigenous population on remote reserves across the continent.

Although most Indigenous Nations are supportive of each other and advocate for common rights and sovereignty, each nation faces its own unique forms of oppression which demand its own resources and energy to fight. This makes it challenging to unify as one powerful voice since much energy and focus and attention must be used on regional issues.

Coupled with the lack of amplification, is also a general lack of power and resources to properly assert rights and maintain sovereignty when and if the governments of the larger colonial nations choose to overstep their bounds. This also makes it next to impossible for Indigenous Nations to participate in the so-called democratic resolutions that the colonial powers consider essential to resolving the issues (the legal system). There is no reason, besides colonial egoism and self-appointed power, that the contemporary issues between Indigenous Nations and colonial governments or other landowners should not be resolved according to traditional Indigenous ways as opposed to being decided by a colonial judge in the Western fashion.

These issues are compounded by the generational lack of access to education in the colonial systems, leaving Indigenous People and Indigenous Nations under-represented and misunderstood by the majority of colonial descendants or participants in the contemporary colonial societies. What makes the lack of access to education worse is the tragic history of "residential schools" which caused immeasurable trauma and likely irreparable mistrust of not only the colonial school system, social services, and policing, but of all other forms of colonial authorities.

What further complicates the matter and makes it difficult for Indigenous Nations to use their potential collective power is that across each country and across each region within those countries, the treaties and rights that may be in place are different. While some nations and groups have no treaties whatsoever, others have clearly defined treaties that work for them, and others still have treaties that were written over 300 years ago and may not reflect the reality of what is happening or needed in the present day. In the case of these old treaties, we must also question the validity of the treaty and how well informed and understanding the people were who signed the treaties. The issues that are arising for Indigenous Nations are all somewhat unique and create fragmentation in the fight for equality.

The truth of the matter is that none of this should matter. The truth is that Indigenous People should not have to fight for their rights to maintain the sovereignty of their territories. The only reason that most Indigenous Nations still have to defend those rights is that the deep-seated racism of colonialism still exists, and although there are treaties that recognize the rights of Indigenous People and Indigenous Nations, the majority of politicians and governments in North America do not. There is still a pervasive and damaging view that Indigenous culture, values, and land use practices are somehow inherently less valid than colonial ways of being and operating. This is likely only because Indigenous culture is not based on capitalism, whereas Western views only see value in something if it is monetized. Indigenous Nations' rights to sovereignty are often respected by governments until there is a motivation or a reason to monetize the land and resources, in which case that need to monetize by default becomes more important than anything that Indigenous Nations are doing there. Governments have a tendency to appropriate land or otherwise override treaty rights and Indigenous Nations sovereignty when they have a monetary incentive of some kind to do so.

Environmental Racism

Another form of systemic racism faced by many Indigenous Nations is environmental racism which has been prevalent since the settlers arrived. Environmental racism can show up in such ways as landfills built on or directly beside Indigenous reserve land or pollutants dumped into waterways on or adjacent to Indigenous Nations communities. This type of racism continues to be extremely physically and mentally harmful to Indigenous Nations people, as is the gaslighting efforts to make believe that it is not discriminatory or race-based decision making that propels these types of decisions.

Environmental racism primarily exists in the form of various levels of government using Indigenous land (or the land adjacent to it) for unwanted and harmful factories or other unsightly usages. For example, if a city wants to build a new landfill rather than situating the landfill in an area where white settlers live, they will use the land on or near a reserve instead. This amounts to the "not in my backyard mentality" where more wealthy and privileged groups of society export their waste and harm to poorer and otherwise disadvantaged groups. The same thing happens globally, where richer countries will have goods produced in poorer countries and leave them with harmful waste and pollution to deal with.

Examples of this can be seen across the continent and over the entire history of colonization. This excerpt from an article by Sezin Koehler (Koehler, 2017) describes a historical example of the type of racist practices that used and manipulated the environment to disadvantage and abuse Indigenous peoples:

While the term environmental racism has only existed for the past few decades, its reality has existed since the beginning of white settler colonialism in the United States and indigenous communities have been particularly victimized by environmental racism.

From 1872 to 1873 the US military went on a targeted campaign to kill millions of buffalo in order to starve Indigenous populations and force them to comply with the newly developing reservation systems. These plots of reservation lands displaced Indigenous communities from their ancestral homes and were often inhospitable environments without easy access to water, food, and other natural resources that made self-sufficiency virtually impossible. Even today, indigenous peoples in America continue to survive ongoing and often daily assaults on their rights to livable spaces.

In the same article, Koehler describes how present-day and ongoing policies continue to affect the health and outcomes of Indigenous peoples in the United States (Koehler, 2017):

Reservation lands are often used by big businesses for the transportation of and also dumping of toxic wastes, which poison what little groundwater there may be and make these areas even less habitable than they already are. Some of the bigger cases of toxic waste dumping and the social repercussions on Native communities have even been brought by various tribes such as the Navajo and Hopi Nations to international fora such as the United Nations and World Health Organization since there is so little being done by America's own government to protect indigenous peoples.

Another big example of this is what is occurring now with pipelines both in the United States and in Canada. Governments are continuing to use Indigenous reserve land, or unceded territory land to build pipelines. Despite the treaties and the vehement protests on the part of Indigenous Nations. These practices deteriorate not only the living environment for people on reserves but the natural environment as a whole.

Indigenous nations have continuously been bullied, marginalized, and treated as second-class citizens. Over the past 500 years, European explorers, traders, settlers, and the newly formed settler nations that they created in North America have continuously dominated Indigenous Nations and used various tactics to acquire land and resources. They have also shown time and again that they do not respect or care about the welfare or sovereignty of Indigenous People by ignoring universal morality along with adamant protests and expressed wishes for sovereignty and land use, even on treaties and unceded territories. To be treated with such disregard repeatedly over time, as Indigenous Peoples have been in North America by all governments that have been in power in all the countries on the continent, degrades the sense of self-worth.

Environmental racism has caused so many impacts to the culture and lifestyle of Indigenous People; from altering traditional land-use practices such as seasonal migration, to loss of habitat of animals that were once relied upon, to a lack of access to clean water, to degradation of the environment limiting agriculture and hunting, to pollution in the water and on the land.

Sovereignty

Sovereignty is perhaps the most important aspect of Indigenous Peoples' rights and a large part of the discussion and conflicts when it comes to relations between many Indigenous Nations and governments.

What is sovereignty and why is it so important for Indigenous Peoples' rights? Sovereignty refers to a nation's autonomy and its ability to self-govern without interference from other nations or external forces, also known as a right to self-determination. Many Indigenous Nations in North America have been advocating and working toward sovereignty since treaties were first created in the 1600s.

Indigenous Peoples are not Canadian or American, they are a separate political and cultural group who live on the same continent and within the borders of the countries, but they are not part of the country. Their territories and reserves are not part of the dominant settler country. As mentioned above many, but not all, Indigenous Nations have an agreement of some kind with the government, and those that do not are entitled to sovereignty by default, as they have never ceded or agreed to give up any of their rights and freedoms as individual nations. Most have signed agreements to maintain the right to determine how their territory or reserve land is used, including a right to consent to potential resource extraction or other projects like pipelines.

Sovereignty usually comes into question when governments wish to use recognized or unceded traditional Indigenous territories. Much more often than not, settler governments use the Indigenous Peoples' land in whatever way they choose without consulting with or gaining prior consent from Indigenous groups that will be affected. In recent times, this has meant the construction of pipelines through and adjacent to Native Reserves and in such a way that will permanently alter the ecosystem and affect the water supply.

Pipelines have been a major conflict between many Indigenous Nations and the governments that have given rise to much discussion about Indigenous sovereignty in North America. Indigenous Nations are generally opposed to the construction of pipelines because the process of constructing them is very disruptive and harmful to the natural environment, not to mention the risk of leaks and spills which cause further harm. When it comes to governments and multinational companies choosing pathways for the proposed pipelines, in true colonial form, the environmental racism shows itself clearly as they are often proposed to cross on or near Native Reserves or unceded territories.

Both in the United States and in Canada, Indigenous Peoples have been fighting against appropriated land use by the federal governments for the construction of pipelines. These fights are very difficult as the settler legal system is very expensive to participate in and oftentimes the group with the most money will be able to drain the resources for the other groups by stalling and creating more work for their lawyers to do. Oftentimes, the groups with less money are not able to compete in the legal system against the richer corporations or governments, so they are never truly held accountable. This is a bully tactic.

In the past, governments would not have consulted at all with Indigenous Nations about land use, and historically treaties were essentially created and used by settlers and governments to secure their own access to resources. That mentality continued over the past few centuries and would continue today if it were not for strong protests and advocacy for the rights of Indigenous Nations and for international organizations like the United Nations. Up until recently, there was never any mention of proper consultation of the Indigenous Nations that might be affected by development or extraction on or near their territories. Now, the standard has become a consultation with Indigenous Nations; although in several contemporary cases the consultation led nowhere, and governments went ahead with development regardless of the input of Indigenous Nations.

This is where the question of sovereignty really comes up because in these circumstances it is clear that the governments are interfering with the ability of Indigenous Nations to determine the use of their land and territories. There is much debate nationally and internationally about how to resolve these issues and what the "best practices" are for governments on how to consult with and gain consent for projects that may be affecting Indigenous Nations.

In more recent decades, the United Nations has been involved in resolving conflicts between Indigenous Peoples and governments. Across the globe, countries that have a colonial history are experiencing similar issues of government dominance and lack of respect for Indigenous rights and freedoms. The dominant colonial powers have a very hard time facing the fact that they have been overstepping boundaries and taking advantage of Indigenous groups for centuries to gain access to resources or lands they want. Now, due to several factors, including being faced with increasing resistance from Indigenous Nations and non-Indigenous protesters, which have become more visible and amplified due to non-commercial or grass-roots media sources on the internet and social media, it has become less acceptable to behave that way and governments are being forced to reflect upon their actions and are starting to be held more accountable.

Originating in 1987, the United Nations (UN) has created a manual for governments and project managers that outlines the minimum requirements of consultation with Indigenous Nations regarding the use of land that may affect them. This is called Free Prior and Informed Consent (FPIC). Essentially, the FPIC document, which is considered an internationally binding law for members of the United Nations, outlines what it means and when, how, and what is required to provide the proper information to Indigenous Nations. It also outlines how to receive informed consent from Indigenous groups before working on a project. Here is a description of FPIC found on the UN website:

FPIC is a principle protected by international human rights standards that state, 'all peoples have the right to self-determination and—linked to the right to self-determination'—'all peoples have the right to freely pursue their economic, social and cultural development'. Backing FPIC is the United Nations Declaration on the Rights of Indigenous Peoples (UNDRIP), the Convention on Biological Diversity, and the International Labour Organization Convention 169, which are the most powerful and comprehensive international instruments that recognize the plights of Indigenous Peoples and defend their rights. (United Nations Department of Economic and Social Affairs Indigenous Peoples, 2016, para 2)

The UNDRIP states clearly that sovereignty and a right to self-determination is a human rights that must be fostered, maintained, and protected. Many Indigenous Peoples, including those in North America, have been taken advantage of and have had their basic human rights trampled by bully colonial states. This is why an international governing system is important as a check and balance to federal powers.

Although UNDRIP, which contains the FPIC principles, is essential as a stepping stone to Indigenous Nations sovereignty, in the eyes of many people, it does not go far enough to truly foster and establish sovereignty and self-determination for Indigenous groups. The document describes informed consent, but in most real-world situations, the governments and companies will move forward with projects regardless of whether Indigenous groups support it or not. When this happens, due to the legal process and cost involved, there is generally very little that can be done to stop it.

CHAPTER 7

GENOCIDE, CULTURAL GENOCIDE, AND INTERGENERATIONAL TRAUMA

There is a form of violence and oppression called 'cultural genocide,' which is the deliberate attempt to eradicate a specific group by cultural means. This means attempting to eliminate language, spiritual practices, and other traditional ways of life. Assimilation practices carried out by colonial governments are considered cultural genocide. The desire and attempts to eliminate Indigenous culture have been very well documented over the history of colonialism. For example, the "anti-Indian" laws created in the 1800s across North America which forbade Indigenous People from holding culturally significant ceremonies and spiritual practices.

Another strong example of the cultural genocide faced by Indigenous Peoples is the treaties and confinement to living on reserve land. For many Indigenous Nations (though not all), the change of lifestyle from moving freely across a vast territory seasonally to hunt was a cornerstone of the lifestyle and having that altered changed many aspects of traditional culture. Further, it left many nations ill-equipped to lead the new sedentary lifestyle, which led to many issues such as inadequate housing and lack of access to water or food sources.

The "residential schools" were established specifically for

95

the purpose of assimilating Indigenous people into the dominant colonial culture by eliminating the ability for children to learn their Native culture. At the time governments assumed that if they taught Indigenous children in a western way, they would become westernized and assimilate into the settler culture.

According to the Merriam-Webster dictionary, 'genocide' is defined as "the deliberate and systematic destruction of a racial, political, or cultural group" (2014). The overall treatment of Indigenous Peoples in North America unquestionably amounts to a cultural genocide; and sadly, there are many cases where the treatment also amounts to genocide.

Examples of genocidal practices in North America are not as common as the cultural genocide, which continues to occur to this day. Some argue that genocide must be intentional mass killings of a cultural group, such as what happened in the Holocaust. Certainly, the type of conquering and mass killings carried out in the 1500s by the Spanish conquistadors is genocide. However, practices like withholding access to food in order to either cause death or to pressure a nation into agreeing to and signing a treaty is akin to genocidal practice.

It's hard to imagine the level of racism that Indigenous People have faced, generation after generation, for over 500 years now. It's important to know that this type of trauma compounds and evolves over time and is affecting every aspect of life, making it increasingly difficult for those who are victims of colonial racism and discrimination to take action to change it. It is a multifaceted and extremely complex situation. If we can view the natural world in terms of cause and effect, or equal and opposite reactions, it is likely that however long Indigenous Peoples have been facing this racist discrimination, is how long it would take the future descendants to recover from it.

"Residential and Boarding Schools"

Arguably, "residential schools" have had the most impact on the lives of Indigenous People. Of course, the "schools" were a form of systemic cultural genocide. The fact that this practice was so accepted and systemized shows how deep the anti-Indigenous sentiments were, and how much it has been a part of the mainstream culture in North America.

Shortly after the point of contact, as Europeans were creating more permanent settlements and colonies, various Christian church groups began operating mission schools. These schools were attended by Indigenous children and adults on a voluntary basis. In the early days of European colonialism, many Indigenous Nations worked closely and amicably with the settlers and wanted to learn more of the European languages and culture. In that time, from the early 1600s to the early 1800s, Indigenous People were not forced to attend the mission schools, nor were they expected to discontinue their Indigenous lifestyles if they did so.

In the northern regions of the continent, it was more common for some Indigenous Nations and European settlements to have closer relationships. This led to many Indigenous People marrying settlers and, as mentioned previously, this even created the distinct Métis Nation as a result. At that time, there was a general acceptance of each other's cultures and an openness to cooperate and learn from each other. Many Indigenous People and families chose to go to the mission schools and to partake more in the settler's culture. Due to the Christian education that was taught at the mission schools, many Indigenous People converted to Christianity from that point on, and many still identify as

Christian to this day.

Although the mission schools do not have a particularly violent or abusive legacy (although it is entirely possible that mistreatment did occur at these schools as well), many people of Indigenous and European descent still consider them to be overall a part of the practice of cultural genocide as they were intended to alter the culture and belief system of Indigenous People.

It wasn't until after the colonies formed their own distinct nations and governments that "anti-Indian" laws and acts were introduced. At the time, the European colonies and settlements were growing larger and more populous. This led to more conflicts about territory boundaries, land use, and rights and access. The settler and colonial governments of the time believed that the answer to the continuous conflicts would be to eliminate the cultural differences by forcing Indigenous People to assimilate into the dominant culture.

Many laws were created in the 1800s to ban Indigenous cultural practices such as spiritual ceremonies. In an effort to further destroy Indigenous culture and assimilate the people, both the American and Canadian governments decided to take over the school system from the missionaries and created state-run "residential" or "boarding" schools. Children were seized from their homes and moved into the schools, some of which were very far from their Native communities, making it impossible for the families to visit.

Although established through the federal governments, like the mission schools, the so-called "residential" and "boarding schools" were still run by Christian religious institutions such as the Catholic church and other similar organizations.

According to first-hand accounts, and the limited school records, the children who attended the schools were malnourished, lacked access to proper healthcare, and were emotionally, physically, and sexually abused. Many of the children died while in the custody of the schools and the families were never informed of their deaths, the children simply never returned.

Another traumatic impact on Indigenous Peoples that came from the tragic legacy of the "residential" and "boarding schools" was caused by the interruption of family-oriented learning and attachment. The Indigenous children taken from their homes never had the opportunity to be loved and cared for by their families, and thereby also never learned how to love and care for families of their own. The interruption to the social learning of loving and parenting skills occurred repeatedly over generations; parenting skills and socio-family learning were not able to occur for over 150 years.

The multifaceted traumas that the "residential" and "boarding schools" caused have created a deep-seated distrust of all authority and especially colonial power, a depleted sense of self-worth—resulting in many mental health-related illnesses such as depression and substance misuse, the decimation of family skills, learned patterns of abuse—as opposed to learned patterns of care and love, and the list continues from there. With each generation being affected by their own experiences and by the experiences of the generations before them, the legacy and trauma continue.

It was not until 2021 that the yards of the former "residential schools" were excavated and the remains of thousands of children were discovered. Sadly, the remains have been found in mass graves and the children are unmarked and virtually unidentifiable. It may be possible for genetic testing to be done and children to be identified. The remains that are identifiable through matching records are being transported back to their home communities and families so that they may be honored and laid to rest with the dignity and love that they deserve. This goes a long way to helping the families of the missing children, the "residential school" survivors, and the descendants of the "school" survivors get some closure. However, the trauma will take many generations to heal, and that is only if the victims are adequately supported to heal.

CONCLUSION

In the eyes of western science, there is no clear date for when the first people arrived on the continent known as North America today. However, it is clear through both western and Indigenous ways of knowing that they arrived over 15,000 years ago. The mysterious beginning of humanity in North America still motivates archeologists and anthropologists to search for the precise answers of how and when people arrived.

For the better part of the 20th century, the Bering Land Bridge seemed to be the most likely way that people first made their way to North America. It was believed that as the ice, which during the Ice Age covered virtually the entire surface of the Earth, began to recede about 12,000 years ago, people from Siberia were able to walk across the span that separates Asia from North America. This area is now filled with water and called the Bering Strait. According to the Bering Land Bridge theory, the Indigenous Peoples came to North America 12,000 years ago in the North and gradually migrated to the South.

However, it is now believed, though challenging to confirm scientifically, that people were actually able to inhabit the Bering Land Bridge throughout the Ice Age period as well. Furthermore, with more scientific technology becoming available—for example, genetic and chronological testing of remains—it has been confirmed that there were people in North America before the time the Ice Age ended. Tests of remains in many parts of the continent and in South America have proved that there have been people in many parts of the continent as far back as 16,000 years ago.

What is very interesting, and also debunks the Bering Land Bridge theory as the first and only way that people came to inhabit North America, is that genetic tests have confirmed several distinct heritage lines in the remains of the ancient Indigenous Peoples of North America. Archaeological evidence, such as types of tools used in various parts of the ancient Americas, also supports the fact that people in North America have more than one common ancestor.

Many scientists are now convinced that at least some groups of people came to North America by boat following what is called the "Kelp Highway." The Kelp Highway is the term used to refer to the ancient aquatic ecosystem that flourished along the shoreline that spanned between Asia and North America. It is believed that this thriving ecosystem would have been able to sustain humans as they traveled and explored by sea, eventually landing on the Pacific Coast and dispersing from that arrival point.

Most Indigenous Nations have origin stories that are considered accurate and completely meaningful in terms of needing to know where the people came from. In the Indigenous way of knowing, there is no need for scientific evidence to support the stories; however, in many cases, the scientific evidence is supportive of the origins and creation stories that have been told and retold by Indigenous knowledge keepers since time immemorial.

Whichever way people first came to the Americas is ultimate of little import. What is known is that for thousands of generations, people have evolved in many diverse ways on this continent. Although each Indigenous group is distinct, what is common to all is that they evolved to live in ways that were completely connected with their unique environment and climate. They each evolved in an organic way with the natural world so that the Indigenous way of life was deeply connected with the environment. The Indigenous ways of life were also sustainable and although societal structure evolved to varying degrees over the span of time that people have lived on this continent, each culture and society was sustainable in the environment that it was a part of.

In general, traditional Indigenous cultures and views did not include the concepts of excess or waste, and therefore, many issues that face the western world did not exist; environmental responsibility and stewardship were a natural and integral part of existing. Traditionally, humans tended to view themselves as another form of animal and as a part of the Earth, not as a separate creature that should dominate the environment or the animals. Everything produced and consumed in traditional Indigenous lifestyles came from the Earth and would return to the Earth after its usefulness to the people ended. There was no garbage in the traditional Indigenous ways of living.

Although there are some basic similarities in the lifestyles of Indigenous Nations in North America, there is also an incredible diversity among the cultures. Each Nation and group had its own histories, traditions, ceremonies, and beliefs. Some traditions and ceremonies were shared between neighboring but distinct groups, such as the potlatches of the Pacific Northwest and the Sun Dances of the prairie and northern groups.

Diversity among nations is also observable in the lifestyles of each Nation. Some Indigenous Nations remained nomadic and migrated seasonally up until European contact and even beyond that. Others were agrarian and semi-sedentary or completely sedentary. While others still, like the Zapotecs, had developed elaborate and complex social structures and city-states.

It is important to recognize this diversity and to be aware that not all Indigenous People share the same history and beliefs. In the North American settler popular narrative of Indigenous People's culture and history, there is a common depiction of Indigenous People as having a particular culture, appearance, and customs. This narrative is not accurate or representative of Indigenous Peoples in reality. It is also the narrative that has led to a romanticized and exploitative view of Indigenous culture, which spreads misinformation about the history of Indigenous Nations, which is both harmful and insulting.

Just as diverse as the cultures and histories of Indigenous Peoples in North America are the contemporary issues that they may or may not face as a result of colonialism. Where some Nations may have had favorable outcomes and are content with their contemporary situation in the context of colonialism and modernity, others may be experiencing many poor outcomes as a result of colonialism. It is also important not to make an assumption of either experience, but to research and possibly ask members of a Nation about the background and the present-day situation and sentiments of the individuals and the Nations.

Although each person and each Nation has had unique experiences, some events have undoubtedly had a grave effect on the majority of Indigenous People in North America and should be approached with the utmost sensitivity, respect, and awareness of the trauma experienced. The "residential" and "boarding schools" are undoubtedly the most impacting colonial practice. With the schools being established in the 1830s and the last school operating up until the 1990s, many victims are still alive and almost every Indigenous person is either a survivor or is a direct relative of a survivor of the "residential" or "boarding schools." In addition to those who have survived, many Indigenous families have stories and memories of the children who never made it home from the "residential" or "boarding schools"; a fate that is so unjust and unimaginable for any parent, sibling, or relative of a missing child to have to accept.

Politically, the Indigenous Nations in North America are in diverse positions as well. Some Nations live in their traditional territories and have never ceded their claim or right to their ancestral land. Some Nations have treaties that were signed hundreds of years ago, while others still have treaties that were created in the past 50 years. Of these Nations, some are thriving while others may not be regardless of their treaty and status in the eyes of the federal governments. There are many factors that determine the outcomes and well-being of Indigenous Nation communities aside from their political relationship with the settler government and country. Including their own Nation's government and politics as well as the geographic situation of their territory and the access to resources and services that support health and well-being.

Despite the diversity of the politics of each individual nation, there are some overarching issues that many Nations face, and that most Nations collectively accept as affecting Indigenous Peoples as a whole. The right to sovereignty and self-determination is the most impacting contemporary issue and conflict between Indigenous Nations and settler governments coupled with multi-national companies. This matter has required a loud and dedicated protest over decades to be recognized and heard, and although some progress has been made in the past 20 years or more, it is still an ongoing and hard-fought battle.

Environmental and land use issues are also a major area where Indigenous sovereignty continues to be denied. When companies and governments want to build or extract on ancestral Indigenous lands and territories, there is often little that Indigenous Nations can do to stop them. The legal system, which in the dominating settler culture would be considered the appropriate way to explore the matter of land use and to seek justice, is exclusive and inaccessible to all but those who have deep monetary resources. When the very system allegedly designed to determine what is just and lawful is based on exclusivity and disadvantages those who are not economically able, can it be considered a way to seek justice? This is perhaps a question that is beyond the scope of this book, but in the context of Indigenous Nations and their relationship with settler culture and government, it seems necessary to pose and to reflect upon.

Such documents as FPIC and UNDRIP begin to approach what may be considered justice for Indigenous Peoples worldwide, but have been shown to be weak in practice. Especially when nations and multinational companies may not face any real repercussions for not following the FPIC principles. There is also criticism that even if the principles are respected and followed, they do not go far enough to protect the right to self-determination that Indigenous Peoples are entitled to as a basic human right.

Other contemporary issues worth noting stem from the outcomes that Indigenous People face due to cultural misunderstanding and prejudice on the part of the members of the dominant culture. This leads to assumptions about individuals that may be based on an incorrect portrayal of Indigenous culture in media, in history books, and courses that are written or taught from the western viewpoint.

Another aspect of the misunderstanding of the Indigenous culture is the unrealistic portrayal of Indigenous Peoples and cultures in the media as well as cultural appropriation of Indigenous culture. Many of the books, movies, and TV shows that portray Indigenous People and culture use western stereotypes, which creates a type of caricature of Indigenous people and culture. This is harmful because it reinforces beliefs about Indigenous People that are not true, and it influences the way the members of the dominant culture view Indigenous People.

Cultural appropriation refers to people from a dominant culture using stories, costumes, or other aspects of Indigenous culture as a selling point for their work. This can happen in many forms, for example, Halloween costumes of the westernized concept of the traditional Indigenous dress. These are offensive, as it is demeaning to the culture and to the people to be portrayed as a costume. It also means that a company is profiting off of selling the (inaccurate and demeaning) portrayal of the traditional Indigenous dress. There are several issues here, including that for hundreds of years Indigenous People have been subject to many forms of abuse and prejudice for their cultural practices and have had to fight continuously to maintain the culture. For a company to now be profiting from that is disrespectful to Indigenous People as it is trivializing the entire colonial experience of Indigenous Peoples.

With advocacy and intentional effort to take back control

of the narrative of Indigenous culture and history, this is slowly changing. Now more shows, films, and media are being made by Indigenous artists and entrepreneurs. It is always good for non-Indigenous people to consume and support Indigenous artists and their work. By watching shows or movies made by Indigenous filmmakers, non-Indigenous people gain a more accurate understanding of Indigenous culture. Supporting Indigenous artists also means that they will be profiting directly from their work and from representing their culture and perspective, rather than a non-Indigenous person profiting from Indigenous culture.

Although there is a long way to go, for many people this is an important era with newfound hope for reconciliation and healing of colonial wounds and trauma. As non-Indigenous people are becoming increasingly aware of a more accurate history of colonialism in North America, it has broadened the discussion and awareness of the issues and racism that Indigenous Peoples have faced. It is only with true understanding and awareness that reconciliation may begin. It requires a continuous openness to learning and understanding to move past the dark history of colonialism and move forward with respect and dignity for everyone.

NATIVE AMERICAN HERBALISM

Improve Your Health, Wellness & Vitality with Indigenous Healing Practices, Medicinal Plants, Natural Herbs, & Herbalist Remedies

HISTORY BROUGHT ALIVE

INTRODUCTION

Herbalism is the science and art of using the natural healing power of plants to make people better and improve their overall health. They are used in traditional healing, used as the base of pharmaceuticals, and their healing powers have been used since ancient times.

Native Americans have traditional practices that stretch back thousands of years. Their ancient cultures were some of the most sophisticated in the whole world. The natural environment in the Americas was in pristine condition when Europeans arrived because Native American cultures learned how to live sustainably with the Earth. They were able to use the natural environment to provide for all their needs, including medicine. This book contains some valuable insights into the Native American medicinal culture.

- Tips about how to grow your herbs.
- Discovering the right herbs for your medicines.
- How to keep them preserved and usable.
- The importance of high-quality herbs when using them for medicinal purposes.

A sizable portion of the book will cover information about searching for plants that you're going to use in your medicinal preparations. safety information—selecting herbs that are healthy and viable—knowing about the different parts of plants so that you can more accurately identify herbs.

CHAPTER 1

FUNDAMENTALS OF NATIVE AMERICAN HERBALISM

Herbalism is the use of plant-based therapies to improve your overall health. It focuses mainly on using the medicinal properties of herbs to both boost your health and overcome diseases or ill health. The Native American nations have perfected the use of herbs for health benefits for more than a thousand years. In recent times, the benefits of natural healing have become a more popular subject of study. Many of the verbal traditions about herbal medicine and practices carried down for generations are now written down so that anyone in the world may benefit from them. This chapter will teach you about some of the basics you need to know to become adept at using herbs in your daily life.

What Is a Herb?

A herb is a plant, of course. But, how is a herb different from any one of the other thousands and thousands of plants in the world?

The first differentiating factor between herbs and other plants is that it refers to plants that are green and leafy. When looking at a herb, both its stems and leaves are normally green. The shapes of the leaves, the stems, and the general appearance of a herb can vary quite a lot. Some might have hairy stems and leaves, while others have smooth ones. The texture of the leaves, the flowers, the way the roots look, and many other parts of one herb might look completely different from another. But there's consistency in the fact that the stems and leaves of a herb are green.

Another quality that separates herbs from other plants is that it's used for flavor. It can be added to foods to change how they taste. It can be added to drinks to alter their flavor. And it can be mixed in with sauces to enhance their flavors. Herbs are known to be more flavorsome than other plants, thus you will often see them used in a kitchen. Additionally, they are known to have an aromatic scent. When smelled directly or crushed, they exude fragrant smells that are pleasant to the nose.

An herb varies from a vegetable in that a vegetable is used as one of the main parts of a dish. An example of this is spinach. Although spinach is a green and leafy plant, its leaves aren't used in small quantities to enhance the flavor of a dish. Rather, they are used as one of the main constituents of a meal for nutritional purposes and to make you feel full. A herb like a dill, on the other hand, is used in small amounts to contribute to the flavor of dishes like fish or potato bakes.

Herbs vary from spices too, even though they're both used in small amounts to flavor dishes. Spices come from plants or parts of plants that aren't green and leafy. Examples of this are the bark, seeds, twigs, berries, and roots. An example of this is cinnamon, which is made from bark. By throwing it into a curry or adding it to a sweet dish, you can alter the flavor of what you're making completely. But it doesn't come from a leafy green plant with green stems.

One last quality of a herb that can separate it from other plants is that it can have medicinal effects. The next section will explain how this occurs.

What Is Herbal Medicine?

Herbal medicine is the use of herbal plants for healing purposes. These medicines come in various forms. This includes tinctures, dried and crushed herb powders, and herbal teas. Herbs contain various compounds that have effects on the body and its parts. Some herbs, for example, can increase your heart rate while others slow it down. By ingesting the suggested or prescribed herbs, your body will function to overcome undesirable conditions. Many of these herbs will bring about long-term changes in your body's health when consistently consumed as directed.

Herbs aren't just "pseudo-healing" as many doctors and practitioners of traditional commercial medicine make it out to be. Modern pharmacology is largely based on herbs and the compounds found in them. While these compounds might have been isolated by the pharmacological industry to the exclusion of other compounds in a given herbal plant, they are still validly gotten into the body for healing purposes when the herb itself is ingested. The modern medical and pharmacological industries would be nowhere near as effective as they currently are but for the contribution of herbs.

Herbal medicine is a holistic approach to healthcare. While the commercial medical industry normally approaches patient healthcare by focusing on handling symptoms that are present, a herbal medicine practitioner takes inventory of the whole person. Diagnosis by herbal medicine professionals takes symptoms into account, but also adds other aspects of the patient's body and mind into account. In this way, the professional gets a full picture of the patient's health, allowing them to improve the patient's overall condition.

There are different herbal medicine traditions in different

parts of the world. There is Chinese herbalism that focuses on restoring the patient's qi energy to optimal levels. Qi is the life force that's believed to circulate through the patient. Chinese herbalism also focuses on bringing balance to the yin and the yang in the body. The yin and yang are said to be the lower and upper parts of the body and the various forces that can affect the body when they're unbalanced. By bringing the two forces into balance, it is believed that any diseases in the body will cease to affect the patient. In other words, Chinese herbal medicine seeks to balance the qi and the forces of yin and yang within the body.

Western herbalism focuses more on the effects different herbs have on systems within the patient's body. It matches diseases and symptoms with a herb that's shown itself to have counteracting effects. It looks at the whole body and notes any system or parts of the body that aren't functioning at normal levels. A range of herbs is prescribed to remedy all body parts and systems not functioning to the required level or that are over-functioning. While this systematic approach focuses on specific symptoms and conditions, the whole patient is still taken into account by taking note of all symptomatic areas.

Unani Tibb is another example of a herbal medicine tradition prescribed to a large population of the world. It refers to the natural healing of Greek origin that's practiced in India, the Middle East, and a few other countries in the region. A balance is sought between the four main liquids and qualities in the body because imbalances are believed to cause diseases. Means such as healthy eating, clean water, and the use of specific herbs are pursued to improve the health of the patient.

These various herbal medicine traditions are systems used to predictably heal patients with various herbs. There are differences between each tradition, but there are also similarities between each tradition that ties herbalism into a single overall field. Native American herbalism links in with other herbal healing traditions from around the world in that it guides how to use herbs to improve the health of the body. It's most similar to Western herbalism because it uses the healing properties of herbs to handle specific symptoms and conditions that are observed. However, there are many legends, religious beliefs, and spiritual elements incorporated into its practice.

In the next section, there will be a description of some of the main differences between conventional medicine and herbal medicine.

How Is Herbal Medicine Different From Conventional Medicine?

Conventional medicine is the medicine you're prescribed when you visit a doctor that's part of the medical association of your state, country, or region. They would have completed a degree and residency covering the use of conventional surgery, medical, and pharmacology practices. Practitioners of conventional medicine normally have very little experience with herbs and plants in a medicinal context. They're used to using processed medications that have been produced by pharmaceutical companies. The three main differences between conventional medicine and herbal medicine are diagnosis methods, the use of the whole plant, and the way that herbs are combined.

Diagnosis under herbal medicine is holistic and looks to find root causes for conditions a patient is experiencing. The herbal medicine practitioner will hear what the main complaints of the patient are and determine if they find any signs of a common underlying condition. Herbs will be prescribed for this underlying condition. Furthermore, the professional will take note of any ailments and other symptoms present in the patient to prescribe herbs for these as well. Finally, a clinical examination (i.e. a direct examination of the patient) will be performed to determine if any other conditions are present. The patient will also be directed to take herbs for these.

Whole plant use refers to herbal medical practitioners either getting the patient to take whole herb plants or medicines that were made by use of the whole herb (such as tinctures). The herb is left unpurified, meaning there aren't parts of the plant that are removed, i.e. leaving the plant whole for medicinal purposes. Unpurified doesn't refer to the cleanliness of the plant—it must be clean, disease-free, and hygienic. Part of the reason the whole plant needs to be used is that then the patient gets the benefits of all the parts of a plant. For example, there might be different benefits available from the flower than from the leaves.

Two underlying guidelines that are actioned by using the whole of the plant for medicinal purposes are 'buffering,' and 'synergizing.' Buffering refers to reducing any effects from toxic parts of a plant by having non-toxic parts of the plant safeguard against a concentration of toxic content. Synergizing is where the different parts of a plant work together to create a positive effect on the body that wouldn't have occurred if each plant part had been used separately. It takes advantage of joining the healing qualities of the plant's constituent parts together.

Finally, combining herbs refers to the practice of using multiple herbs together in one medicine. An example of this is creating capsules of dried and crushed herbs that all tackle the same body issues. In doing this, the herbalist is allowing the patient to have their condition or conditions handled from multiple natural sources. A combination of multiple medicinal substances is called polypharmacy and isn't something available with traditional medicines. Combining herbs has the following benefits:

- synergy
- buffering
- more effective
- lower concentrations of adverse substances.

Synergy is accomplished by having the benefits of multiple types of herbs combined. As with the use of the whole plant where all the parts of a plant synergize their healing potential, the same is accomplished when combining herbs. The benefits of multiple types of herbs are combined for the patient. Buffering is similarly improved by adding multiple types of herbs together, thereby diluting the potential negative effects of any single herb. While potential negative reactions are diluted, the desired positive effect isn't diluted. This is because all the chosen plants in the mix are chosen for the shared health effect they can have on the patient, e.g. lowering blood sugar.

Herb combination is more effective than using a single herb because the same condition is being remedied using multiple sources. Each plant has unique combinations of nutrients and substances. With multiple unique substances working together toward solving the same problem, there's a higher chance of the condition being remedied. Further, none of the substances are too highly concentrated because they're diluted by the other beneficial elements present, which avoids the problem of much of a good thing becoming a bad thing.

Different Types of Herbs

There are five main groups of herbs. These are:

1. Nutritive
2. Bitter
3. Mucilaginous
4. Aromatic
5. Astringent.

Nutritive

Nutritive herbs are herbs that are useful for foods. An example of this is a dandelion leaf. Herbs that fall into this category are green and leafy like other herbs, but they're more properly classified as vegetables for culinary purposes. This is because they are used as the main constituent in meals, rather than in small quantities for flavoring purposes. Other herbs that fall into this classification include alfalfa, nettle, chickweed, and horsetail.

Bitter

Bitter herbs contain substances, such as phenols, that give them a bitter flavor. The substances that give them a bitter flavor are also often the reason why those herbs are capable of healing conditions. Bitter herbs are further broken down into four subcategories. These are:

1. Diuretic herbs
2. Alkaloid containing herbs
3. Saponin containing herbs
4. Laxative herbs.

Diuretic

Diuretic herbs have the effect of helping you urinate easily. When people are experiencing some types of bladder-related conditions, these herbs are very helpful in alleviating discomfort and difficulties. Herbalists prescribe bitter herbs with diuretic effects to ensure that a patient's waste elimination systems work properly. Additional benefits of diuretics are reduced blood pressure (because there's less liquid in your bloodstream), reducing the levels of sodium in your body, and decreasing the amount of water in your body. In conventional medicines, water pills are the solution for this.

Alkaloid

Alkaloid herbs contain substances that have alkaline effects on the body. This means that they counteract acids to create salts (on a chemical level). The result is that your body becomes more alkaline, which in and of itself has health benefits. There are other benefits commonly experienced when taking alkaloids, depending on which one you're taking. These benefits include:

- reducing inflammation in the body
- attacking bacteria
- prevention of mitosis in cells (which is beneficial in reducing the spread of cancer spreading)
- reducing tumor sizes and growth
- aiding with sleep
- improving one's state of mind and mental condition
- general pain relief
- local pain relief.

The list of benefits possible from alkaloids is long and varied. There are natural sources of these benefits (i.e. herbs) as well as artificial sources. Artificial sources have been isolated for use in our daily lives and are now common in our medicines and our foodstuffs. Examples of some of the most common conventional alkaloids are nicotine, atropine (a muscle relaxant), strychnine (a stimulant), morphine, quinine (a substance that can combat malaria), ephedrine (used for hay fever and asthma), and caffeine. Most of these are sourced from plants, but in conventional use, they're isolated from the rest of the plant, resulting in a concentrated quantity of these substances.

Saponins

Saponins form a group of substances that foam when mixed in with water. They are found in many plants, especially in bitter herbs. There are multiple benefits available from consuming saponins, including:

- reduction of kidney stone prevalence
- reducing the occurrence of new tooth cavities and the growth of existing cavities
- lowering blood sugar
- reducing the risk of cancer
- preventing aggregation of blood platelets (i.e. reducing clotting issues)
- remedying lead poisoning
- lowering lipid levels in the blood
- reducing the overabundance of calcium in your urine
- increasing the level at which you absorb other nutrients and health-increasing substances.

There are other benefits of saponins. They can be obtained from a large number of herbs, with over 4,000 plants existing with saponin contents. While they're often bitter, they can be very sweet indeed.

Laxative

Finally, laxative bitter herbs facilitate your bowel movements. In other words, when you're constipated or having trouble defecating, herbs that contain laxative substances can help. The benefits don't stop at improving your bowel movements. Other benefits of bitter laxative herbs include:

- killing parasitic worms
- protection of your liver (both in terms of function and

general health)

- improving the health of your mucus membrane (reducing inflammation, preventing build-up, and lowering levels of discharge)
- combating fevers
- purifying your blood, thereby improving the health of multiple systems throughout your body
- better secretion of saliva
- improving the flow of bile from the gallbladder to the small intestine, thereby improving overall digestion
- alternative effects, i.e. overall improvement of your health.

Mucilaginous

Mucilage is a sticky substance secreted by a plant or other living organism. In the case of a plant, the secretion is made up of multiple sugar molecules and substances bound together as one. An example of this is the sticky substance you find around chia seeds when you've soaked them in water. Mucilage is usually used either as an adhesive or for medicinal use, such as soothing the mucus membranes.

Mucilaginous herbs produce mucilage to help heal and improve various bodily systems. They are typically consumed with water or mixed with water to fulfill their functions fully (whether used internally or externally). This allows the herb to absorb the water and bulk out into a soft, wet, sticky mass. The mass is what produces the positive effects herbalists use mucilaginous herbs for. The list of benefits for this type of herb is very long, with some of them being:

- soothing your skin
- softening skin
- hydrating dry skin
- reducing inflammation (of mucus membranes, organ

linings, and nerves)

- hydration (by combining with water and allowing for easy absorption of water into the body)
- thickening out your stool, allowing the alimentary canal to move and process things you've consumed effectively
- absorbing toxins in the intestines and carrying them out with your stool
- making your bowel transit time faster (i.e. increasing the speed with which food moves through your digestive system
- protecting the lining of your stomach from gastric acid
- relaxing your intestine
- reducing spasms in your lungs (which in turn reduces coughing), urinary tract, intestines, and spinal muscles
- protecting the tissues that line your organs and the tissues that make up the many membranes in your body
- reducing pain and irritation in membranes and protective tissues
- healing wounds.

With the benefits available from mucilaginous herbs, it's worth knowing what the most important ones are and the benefits available with each.

Aromatic

Aromatic herbs get their name from smelling pleasant. Their pleasant scent results in them often being used in perfumes and for flavoring foods. Lemon grass is one such herb. These herbs are also widely used for their medicinal properties. Medicinal properties abound with these herbs, being concentrated around improvements in energy and improvements in the conditions of your nerves. These two subcategories of healing aromatic herbs are classified as stimulants and nervines.

Stimulants

Most of us have heard of stimulants by this point in time. They consist of a category of herbs, medicines, and substances that are known to produce energy or the speed of various functions in your body. Coffee is a non-herb example of a stimulant. To break down the function of stimulants into a more detailed overview, stimulants increase the activity in your organs. Specific body systems that are boosted are the circulatory, digestive, and respiratory systems.

Nervines

A nervine herb heals your nerves, causing your body to feel soothed. This has a positive effect on your whole body because nerves affect how you think, move, and perceive your environment. Nervine herbs are known to be especially good for your circulatory, digestive, and circulatory systems. Thus, both stimulants and nervine herbs have particularly good effects on these three systems, albeit for different reasons.

Astringent

Astringent herbs tighten up the muscles, skin, and other body tissues. This is achieved by causing water to be pulled out of the tissue, thus causing it to shrink. Astringents are popular for cosmetic purposes because they give the skin a more taut appearance and they prevent discharge (such as the discharge of sebum). They do, however, also have important effects on the internal functions of a body when used correctly. Examples of internal benefits that can be obtained from using astringent herbs include:

- killing microorganisms that can cause diseases
- pain relief, especially in the muscles
- balancing the functions within the body for optimal

synergy

- inducing delayed menstruation (when the delay is caused by something other than pregnancy)
- stemming bleeding (both internal and external)
- counteracting the expulsion of a baby from the womb before they're viable.

Now that you know what the five main types of herbs are, we'll look at how you can source your herbs.

Sourcing of Herbs

How and where you source your herbs has a big effect on the quality of the herbal medicine you'll be making. The best quality herbs are generally from wild and undisturbed landscapes reasonably far away from cities. This is because there's little to no pollution and the herbs get adequate nutrition because that's their natural environment. High-quality herbs can, however, be sourced from other places. When grown in greenhouses, for example, the herbs' environment can be adjusted to their preferences—along with very low pollution being present in this environment.

Whatever the source is, there are some indications you can use to determine whether the herbs are of a good enough quality or not. These indications are:

- harvesting techniques
- how they were stored
- drying
- freshness
- labeling.

Harvesting

The way a herb is harvested, and when it's harvested affect the quality of the herb. When the herb is harvested at the correct time of the year and at the correct stage of its lifecycle, it will undoubtedly be of higher quality than a herb that isn't. If you can get information about how a herb was harvested, that's already a good sign. If the person you're buying it from seems confused when you're asking them about harvesting practices for a particular herb or they have no information for you, that's an indication that the herb might not be of the quality you desire.

When you're growing your herbs for medical purposes, make sure that you study harvesting techniques for each herb you're growing. There are general things you need to know, such as how to prune herbs. Then there are things specific to each herb, such as when to harvest. If you know the basics and the specifics of the herbs in your garden or greenhouse, then you'll be capable of producing quality products that are suitable for medicinal purposes.

Storage

When storing your herbs for medicinal reasons, keep the three points of light, oxygen, and temperature in mind. All three of these can damage a herb by breaking down the compounds or structures that make it up. Light breaks down the potency of the herb, essentially washing out the goodness. Oxygen disintegrates the components of a herb by combining with them to form chemical reactions. Further, oxygen also supports microbes in their conquest of your herb stocks, giving them the fuel they need to keep munching away at your precious supplies. Finally, temperature also reacts with the constituents of a herb by causing reactions that break them down.

The method herbs are stored before being dried is also important (if you're making use of dried herbs). Some places will throw the herbs on the ground and leave them there. Or the herbs will be stored in unhygienic conditions or handled by people with unwashed hands. These are examples of storage conditions to avoid between the harvesting and drying stages. After the drying stage, the next important point of storage is how the herb is stored between drying and use.

By heeding the points in the first paragraph concerning light, temperature, and airtight conditions, stocks can be stored for long-term use. To keep oxygen out, make use of glass jars, plastic sealable containers, or tins with an airtight seal. When using plastic and glass, it's best to use a dark-colored holder so that the herbs inside aren't exposed to too much light. Store them in a cupboard or fridge to keep the temperature from rising too high. Keep the temperature below 100 degrees Fahrenheit for optimum preservation.

When you're purchasing herbs from another person or company, ask them about their storage methods. If you find some of their storage practices are sub-par, then you know you won't get the quality of herb you need from them (such as just storing herbs in open bins in a sunny spot). The way they store the herbs when sending or giving them to you is also important. If you're taking some herbs with you from a store, then a paper bag should be good enough. But, if you're ordering online and your herbs are couriered to you, it's best to get a supplier that will send them to you in vacuum-packed plastic bags.

Drying

Drying herbs is important for a herbalist because it's easier to work with dried herbs than with fresh herbs. Both can be used medicinally, but when you use fresh herbs you have to use them up a lot faster and you can't use them in pill or capsule form. Dried herbs can be put into capsules or pills, thus making it easy for a herbalist to keep them in stock for patients. Dried herbs also last very long because there's no moisture for bacteria to live on, thus deterioration of the herb is much slower.

Freshness

If you're buying fresh herbs, they should be fresh, not wilted. They can't be mushy and brown, and they can't have signs of infections. If you notice there are dark spots on it that aren't supposed to be there, then avoid that specimen. If there are light patches, the same thing applies. Don't make use of any herbs that have infestations of bugs or other critters because this is asking for trouble.

The worst thing you can do is get fresh herbs that are planted close to areas that are high in pollution. A stream close to a factory waste site is an example of this. Polluted areas are all too common, so be aware of potential pollution sources so that you only take the healthiest of herbs. Common sources of pollution are commercial farms, factories, busy roads, dumping sites, and densely populated areas. You can find spots with very low pollution close to populated areas, but they will take some searching. Take the time you need to determine the herbs you're sourcing are free from this—your body will thank you for it.

When harvesting fresh herbs, a good sign that it's fresh enough to take is that it's green. The green shouldn't be faded because this shows that it's getting stale or old. It also shouldn't be yellow or pale (unless its description says it's naturally that color). If a herb is saturated with green, then you know it's in a healthy condition. When you feel it, it should be relatively firm, not wilted. To prevent daily influences on herbal freshness and greenness, harvest early in the morning or late in the day so that you don't pluck it during daily evaporation periods. In this way, you're preventing yourself from harvesting wilted plants, which will keep them fresher for longer.

To prevent your herbal supplies from going bad, don't harvest too much. Collect the quantity you need, not the available quantity. In this way, you'll have to keep coming back for more when your supplies are used up. This is far better than using up the amount you expected to use in a period and then making use of stale supplies because you have it in stock. Forcing yourself to harvest in small quantities will keep this problem from happening.

If you're not sure about when a herb was harvested (such as when you're buying it from a store or online), then ask. Most herbal shops will be happy to let you know when they got it from their supplier and when their supplier harvested it. By getting this information, you can make sure that you're not buying a stock that's going to diminish in freshness soon after you buy it. Getting your supplies online works in much the same way. Send the supplier an email or message and ask when they gathered it. This way you can vet the purchases you make so that you don't get old stock. If an online supplier isn't willing to supply this information, then you shouldn't opt into using their product.

Another thing you can do to determine if the stock you're purchasing is fresh is to smell it and taste it. Your olfactory senses are capable of collecting a lot of information when it comes to herbs with distinctive flavors and aromas, so trust those senses. If you can't smell the herb, then it's probably not fresh enough or not of good enough quality to be used. If you can smell it easily and it exudes the type of aroma that it should, then you know it's a good, fresh supply that you can make use of. The same goes for the taste. If it tastes strong and it tastes right, then you can rest assured that it's of a high enough quality to use.

The final point to take into consideration when ascertaining if your herb supplies are fresh is to do your research. A herb might not look right if you don't have enough information about it. Maybe it's spotted, which makes you hesitant to get it. But, when you look at its description, it might show that a spotted color is exactly how it should be. Whatever the case may be, you won't know whether the herb looks, smells, and tastes the part unless you first have reliable information to evaluate it.

Labeling

Checking the labels of products you buy is a good way to make sure you're sourcing produce that's up to standard. The first thing you should look out for is the harvest date. If it's too far into the past, then it's better to avoid it. If it's close to the present, then it should be okay to get it. When you build the habit of checking the harvest date and setting your standards about what's too old, you're taking a good step forward in ensuring your medicines are of a high grade. When there aren't harvest dates available on a label, again, just ask. And if the supplier isn't willing to supply the information, cut your losses and find another supplier.

Your purchase date is also a useful date on the label of the herb's packet or jar. Your supplier won't often note down the purchase date, but it's something you can easily make a note of. The reason this is a useful thing to track is that when you open a packet, you're immediately exposing the herb to environmental factors that can start deteriorating. While the packet stays sealed, there's some level of protection because no new air and no humidity can get in. But, when you open it up, the herb will come into contact with both air and humidity. Setting a window for yourself between opening the herb and using it will be a useful guideline to prevent yourself from using something that's no longer of medicinal value.

How Can I Know if a Particular Herb Will Work for Me?

There are reasons that herbs might not work for you, such as allergies. To make sure the herbs you use will benefit you, you can take the Universal Edibility Test described below. If you don't have time for this test, but you've accurately identified a non-toxic plant, you should first try a small amount before trying any larger amount. This way you can get to your clinic or hospital fast without maximum exposure if you have some sort of reaction.

The Universal Edibility Test

This is a test you can use in any situation to determine if your body will accept a herb or a part thereof. It can even be used in survival situations where you have no reference materials or internet coverage.

Procedure

Break the plant into its constituent parts because some parts might be toxic while others are completely healthy. The constituent parts are the roots, stems, leaves, flowers, fruit, and seeds. Use something to cover your hand while you do this in case the plant can cause contact dermatitis. Make sure it's okay by smelling it. Odd smells aren't a good sign, especially if it smells almond-like or pear-like. These two smells indicate cyanide content. Also, watch out for musty-smelling herbs because there might be mold present.

Perform a touch test by rubbing the part of the plant you're testing on your wrist or inner elbow. If you react, such as getting a rash, burn, or boils, then the test can be concluded as a negative. Otherwise, you should now perform the eating test. Take a small bit of the plant and put it against your lips. If you notice any numbness, prickling, or other undesirable reaction, conclude the test. If not, put a small piece of the plant on your tongue (preferably cooked).

Don't chew the plant piece; just leave it there. If there's a negative reaction such as your mouth watering excessively, conclude the test. If not, chew it but don't swallow it. Chewing will release its juices and you can take note to rule out any further reactions, for example, vomiting. Now swallow the small piece if the test hasn't concluded in a negative thus far. Any negative reactions should once again result in a negative test conclusion, like if you feel your throat becoming swollen.

If there haven't been any reactions yet, now you can cook up a small meal with the plant and eat it. The meal should optimally be cooked because some plants are toxic when raw but non-toxic when cooked. Eat up your meal and wait for any reactions. If there aren't any, you know it's safe to eat that part of that plant species. If there are reactions, you know you shouldn't take any of that plant part in the future.

Time Frames

The test is designed to have eight-hour intervals between each major step. While this is a long period and you'll probably feel very hungry by the time you actually eat, you mustn't skip the timeframes. Cutting them short will put you at risk. The periods are as follows:

- Fast for eight hours.
- Leave eight hours between the touch test and putting it against your lips.
- Fifteen minutes should be allowed between touching the plant material to your lips and putting it in your mouth.
- There should be a fifteen-minute interval between putting it in your mouth and chewing it.
- After chewing, allow fifteen minutes before swallowing
- Wait for eight hours after swallowing to determine

whether there are any reactions or not.

Tips

Fasting first is important as it will rule out any other variables in your system while conducting the test. If you don't fast, you won't know what's causing the reaction in your body, thus making the test unreliable.

If you notice any indications that the plant is inedible, don't even conduct the test on that plant part. The risk isn't worth it in a situation where you can't properly identify and research a plant. Signs of inedibility are discoloration, parsley-like leaves, milky residue (i.e. milky sap), or an indication that there's an infection or infestation. Further, if you have started conducting the test and you have a negative reaction, force yourself to vomit, and then flush out your system with lots of clean water. This way you expel the maximum amount of plant matter out of your body that you possibly can.

Now that you know how to ensure a herb or plant you're going to consume is safe, you'll want to know how long it will take for the herb to prove effective on your body or mind.

How Long Does It Take for Herbs to Be Effective?

It depends on the herb, the person, and the preparation of the medicine. In general, it takes about two to three weeks for any major effects (D'Alberto, n.d.). This is a non-specific average that could vary based on the factors in the first sentence.

How Safe Are Herbs?

Herbs have been used for thousands of years. People wouldn't use something for that long if it only causes harm. There are slight differences in the effects of a herb from person to person, but the effects are largely predictable after centuries of trial and error. Knowing your herbs prevents the situation of using herbs that are unsafe or toxic. Besides knowing herb-specific information about toxicity, you also need to know the safety rules that guide foraging. When you follow these safety rules, you keep yourself safe while gathering herbs, which then allows you to safely test and consume those herbs.

Advantages and Disadvantages of Herbal Medicine

As with anything, both positive and negative effects can be experienced from the use of herbal medicine. Being aware of the positive and negative outcomes helps you take full advantage of herbs. This section contains details of the advantages and disadvantages you might face.

Advantages

Herbal medicine is cheap—it can be home-grown, obtained from health stores, or obtained for next to no cost from nature zones. The expenses for making herbal medicine are low, which means that there will be a low cost. There also isn't a large discrepancy between the demand and supply of herbal medicine since herbs are easily obtainable, resulting in predictable good pricing. As a result, herbal medicine has a lower cost than conventional medicine.

There are fewer side effects than in conventional medicines. The compounds are found in nature. It's generally known which parts of which herbs are toxic, and therefore to be avoided because most herbs have been tried and tested extensively over history. Further, buffering results in less potency of negative effects a herb could give, and synergy results in the joint positive effects of multiple herbs and herb parts.

There's no synthetic content in herbal medicine. There

aren't unnatural chemicals inserted into the medicine. The compounds in herbal medicines are complex and they aren't overly concentrated on one chemical structure, which is a problem you might face with conventional medicine.

Many have antimicrobial effects. This is good for people who have infections, including fungal infections. Even though many herbs are antimicrobial, they aren't harsh on your system like orthodox antibiotics.

Disadvantages

One of the disadvantages is that it can alter the effects of conventional medicines when herbal medication is taken. Thus you should consult your medical practitioner first so that you don't unintentionally cause chemical reactions in your body.

There's a lack of regulation when it comes to herbal medicine. You might end up buying from an unknown seller or a seller that hasn't proved their mettle yet. You don't know if the supplier is keeping to hygiene and quality standards. Normally there's no license required to provide herbal medicine, even if some herbalists voluntarily obtain licenses.

Many herbs haven't been tested as to their side effects on pregnant and breastfeeding women. There are a few that have been shown to make pregnancy and giving birth easier. There are also a few that have been shown to increase lactation. That said, many haven't been tested and some have even caused miscarriages. For this reason, you should always check with your healthcare professional first when you want to take a new herb while pregnant or breastfeeding.

You can't take any herbal medicines for two weeks before surgery. If you do, it might cause complications, particularly when you're under anesthesia. If you did take herbal medicine within the two-week window, you need to let your surgery team know so that they can determine whether it will make the operation unsafe or not.

Elderly people and young children could be put at risk by giving them herbal medicines. This is because dosages might vary due to the undeveloped or frail conditions of their body. Adults generally have more robust bodies, resulting in there not being an issue with taking herbal medicine. But, with the frail bodies of the young and elderly (especially when the elderly are on a host of other medications), a healthcare practitioner should be consulted first as to the intended herb use and dosage.

Myths About Herbal Medicine

In this context, 'myth' refers to unproven beliefs that are widely held. The myths detailed in this section are inaccurate, but by understanding they aren't factual, you can examine the subject of herbalism with more of an open mind.

One myth is that "herbal medicines don't work." They most emphatically do work. They produce potent effects that can help handle or alleviate most conditions that exist. Herbs have been used since before recorded times to improve people's health and still produce miracles that astound modern medicos and scientists.

"Herbal medicine is not researched" is another. This statement is not true. Lack of research by medical faculties and medical researchers doesn't mean that others haven't researched herbs. Herbalists use passed-down knowledge that has been researched and put through trial and error for generations. Modern herbalists contribute to this knowledge with their own experience and trial-and-error research, thereby increasing knowledge for the next generation. The medical industry is slowly but surely catching up. There's much research for them to still conduct, but progress is being made.

Although herbal medicine is cheap, some believe the myth that it's expensive. As covered in the advantages of herbal medicine in the previous section, the idea that it's expensive isn't true. While it might be more expensive than no treatment at all, it's much cheaper than the medicines you'll find in conventional pharmacies.

"Herbs are for hippies" is about one of the most unimaginative myths you can get. All manner of people uses herbal medicine. Hippies didn't exist in the ancient societies where herbal medicine first flourished. They might have incorporated some of it into their subculture during the hippie era of the 1960s, but many other types of people also use it. People that use herbal medicine range from school teachers to billionaire CEOs, and from famous actresses (e.g. Shailene Woodley) to handymen, and beyond. It's a truly global healing culture.

Some believe that herbal medicine is the same as homeopathy. This isn't quite accurate because the specific methodology behind homeopathy is different from herbalism. Homeopathy uses small concentrations of natural substances for healing. These small quantities would produce symptoms of the condition troubling the patient if taken in larger quantities. The purpose of this is to get the body's natural defenses to kick in and face the condition the person is experiencing. Herbalism doesn't make use of this method; the method used in herbalism is detailed in the first chapter.

"Herbs are natural, therefore safe" is another myth. Not all natural things are safe—the poison on a dart frog is natural after all. Some herbs or parts of herbs are toxic, and therefore not safe. Thus, the safety of a herb varies from species to species. You need to know the basic medical information about any given herb to know if it's safe—and there's a lot of information available about herbs when you need it—you can't just wing it.

Safety Information

You can put yourself in harm's way by using herbs in inappropriate ways. Seeking guidance from a professional is the best way around this. If you're using it yourself without professional guidance, do your homework first. Get factual information that you can reliably base your self-medication. Reliable information does not necessarily include opinion pieces about herbs and it doesn't necessarily include advertising pieces for herbal medicines already on the market.

To be safe, make sure your herbs come from a reliable and trustworthy source. There shouldn't be incorrect labeling of the product; mislabeling is a big red flag. Untested commercially sold herbal products are often worse than locally sourced fresh and dried herbs because with the locally sourced herbs you know exactly what you're getting, but with the untested, off-label commercial variety, you don't know exactly what's in the container.

CHAPTER 2
BENEFITS OF HERBAL MEDICINE

We know that herbs provide benefits. People wouldn't keep on using them if benefits weren't obtainable. In this chapter, there will be descriptions of some of the more common benefits you might expect.

Immune System Support

Your immune system can be strengthened by the consumption of herbs. Combining this with spices and a healthful diet gives the best immune system results. Herbs can even build up your immune system against some highly communicable diseases. A weakened immune system results in a predisposition for ill health because you're open to infection. By protecting your immune system, you're less likely to get infections.

Natural Remedy for Menopause

Menopause can be a distressing time for any woman. This is the time when they stop menstruating, and it's a sign of aging that many find discouraging. Indications include hot flashes, some incontinence (loss of bladder control), trouble with sleep, irritability, losing muscle mass, gaining fat, and discomfort during sex.

Diet is important during and after menopause due to great variations of progesterone and estrogen levels causing odd reactions in the body. Herbs contribute to a healthful diet, mitigating potential postmenopausal conditions that can arise, including heart issues, and osteoporosis (brittle bones from lack of vitamin D and calcium). Herbs are available that alleviate the symptoms and the underlying condition. As a result, diet is boosted in the right direction and there is less risk of postmenopausal complications.

Boosted Circulation

Poor circulation results in a lack of adequate blood flow to various parts of your body. It can result in spider veins and can lead to other health complications. The remedy is being active or exercising; at the very least standing up and moving around every hour. Not wearing tight clothing helps, and having herbs that increase the circulation of blood is a long-term solution.

Sharper Memory

Memory is a vital component of our personal and professional lives. Without this skill, we wouldn't be able to keep track of things, people, places, and actions. We have both short-term memory and long-term memory. Short-term memory is used to keep track of things that have happened recently so that we can work from them and refer back to them in our daily actions. Long-term memory is where our embedded knowledge and our life experiences are contained. Many would kill to have a better memory. Herbs can provide just that—not only increasing memory, but also improving other mental faculties, such as focus, alertness, and increased brainpower. Herbs are a great addition to your diet to increase your mental faculties. Some have even been found to assist people with brain disorders

Stress Relief

Stress can be a crippling condition. Our attention goes off

from the work we're doing and we can't concentrate, which in turn increases stress even more. The stress we build up can be about small challenges we keep facing or large life changes, there's no telling what might cause a person stress until it does. We could use conventional medications, but they are harsh on the system and produce many side effects, some of which can be quite strong. Rather than putting yourself through a myriad of potential side effects, make use of natural means. Many herbs have been proven to assist with stress relief. Herbal bitters are a good way to ease stress (bitters are herbs or spices that are concentrated in high-proof alcohol). You can use herbal teas for everyday stress relief.

Stable Energy Source

Many people have varying energy levels throughout the day and week. When you're full of energy, you get a lot done for a few hours; when you have very little energy, you get almost nothing done for the rest of the time.

Balancing out the energy levels for consistency helps a lot—herbs can be used to accomplish this. Multiple other things need to be done to maintain energy levels. They include getting enough sleep, having a healthy diet, doing reasonable amounts of exercise, practicing self-care, and taking necessary supplements. Many herbs have energy-giving and energy-maintaining effects. A lot of energy drinks make use of herbs or phytochemicals in herbs to induce energy surges, such as ginseng.

When taken in the natural form of a herb (rather than artificial means such as energy drinks), the 'rush' is sustained and balanced out, thus lasting throughout the day.

Helps Lower Cholesterol

Cholesterol is a type of lipid found in your body. It's important for multiple functions, including building cells, making hormones, and producing vitamins for your body to use. Your liver makes the cholesterol your body needs, while a lot of animal food products—and a few plant foods high in saturated fats—make your liver produce too much cholesterol.

Cholesterol is needed in small quantities. In large quantities, however, it's bad for you. It forms plaque when it groups with other things in your bloodstream, resulting in blockages of your veins, arteries, and capillaries. If your blood vessels become blocked or restricted, this raises your blood pressure, putting you at risk of a heart attack. Further, the restriction of blood flow prevents your heart from getting all the nutrients and oxygen that it needs to operate optimally. Thus, the fact that many herbs help lower cholesterol is a benefit that can't be overlooked.

Relevant herbs don't only lower cholesterol, but also increase heart health. Heart health results in a heart that beats appropriately and doesn't struggle to function. When a heart struggles to function, it puts a person at risk of death, thus making it a priority to keep your heart healthy. While exercise is a good way of ensuring your heart remains in top shape, herbs provide another layer of heart health improvement that can be invaluable in keeping your body safe. What's more, they can be taken over long periods, thereby ensuring heart benefits from herbs long after you've started taking them.

Elevates Blood Pressure

Many people don't realize it, but low blood pressure can be a problem, just as high blood pressure is. There's an optimal range for blood pressure, depending on your age. If it's too low, you're at risk of heart failure, kidney failure, stroke, and shock, amongst other things. Thus, if it's determined that you're hypotensive (i.e. your blood pressure is too low), you need to take action to heighten it.

The appropriate herbs will help steer your blood pressure upwards so that you're no longer at risk of unwanted medical phenomena. Some herbs that help with low blood pressure are St. John's Wort, licorice (the plant), and ephedra. Combining these herbs with a diet of high salt, frequent small meals, and consumption of electrolytes will help. Even caffeine is of benefit to those with low blood pressure (which can be found in yerba mate).

Helps Control Blood Sugar and Insulin Activity

Blood sugar is the amount of glucose that's present in your blood. It determines the amount of energy you'll have and determines how much energy you can burn.

Too high a level (called hyperglycemia) is caused by an inability of the body to use insulin properly (also known as insulin resistance) or too low a level of insulin produced by the body. This can result in diabetes. Hyperglycemia can also damage your blood vessels, body tissues, and organs (especially your eyes) over the long run. Signs of hyperglycemia include frequent urination, blurred vision, weight loss, feeling very thirsty, weakness, and being tired. Causes of this condition include stress, being unwell, inactivity, too much sugar or starch in your diet, and not taking diabetes medication when instructed to do so.

Too low a level (called hypoglycemia) is also an undesirable condition. Signs include hunger, dizziness, sweating, irritation, anxiety, moodiness, shakiness, tingling lips, being pale, heart palpitations, and tiredness. Longer-term signs include blurred vision, fits, seizures, sleepiness, weakness, passing out, slurred speech, clumsiness, difficulty concentrating, and confusion. The causes for this condition include medicine with too much insulin, alcohol, intense and non-routine exercise, lack of adequate carbohydrates, skipping meals, and delayed meals.

There are ways to optimize your use of insulin, like getting enough sleep, keeping physically active, and getting exercise. Stressing less is something that can contribute to better insulin use, as well as a healthy diet that includes multicolored vegetables as well as fiber. Reducing the consumption of sugar and starch is important when trying to manage insulin levels better. Herbs are also effective tools to handle insulin better. Turmeric, garlic, and ginger are all herbs that can have a positive effect.

Helps Protect Against Cancer

Both very little and vast amounts of information are known about this disease. There are many types of cancer. The condition is basically the propagation of cells that break down the functioning of organs and systems within the body. Conventional medicine gets rid of it using surgery, radiation, and chemotherapy, but even with these treatments, the success rate is very low.

Radiation therapy is very heavy on the body. There are many side effects; side effects that some find unbearable. The side effects a person experiences vary from case to case, depending upon the type of cancer, its location, and other factors. Examples of side effects (depending on where radiation is applied) include nausea, tooth decay, lung scarring, cramping, sexual discomfort, and fertility problems.

Chemotherapy also produces a myriad of side effects, examples of which are fatigue, anemia, bleeding, rough and dry skin, trouble sleeping, difficulty focusing, and fertility issues. It's not very easy to go through these side effects, but the effects are a necessary evil for those who have a cancerous condition and are putting all their effort into overcoming the condition.

Herbal medicine has proven to assist in overcoming cancer in many cases. Multiple herbs have anticancer effects in which tumors are broken down and fought against by the herbal compounds. While there is by no means a guarantee that any given herb will kill cancer, there are also fewer side effects and the side effects are less intense. By familiarizing yourself with the various herbs that combat cancer, you never know whose life you might end up saving. Western and Chinese Herbalism have both proven effective in aiding against cancer in many cases. Be aware that spices are also known to produce anticancer effects and should be considered for therapeutic purposes. Other assistive remedies that have a track record of assisting include using cannabis and flower remedies.

Helps to Reduce Low-Density Lipoproteins

Lipoproteins are important in your body because they carry around important fats and proteins. They are found in the bloodstream and are categorized as either cholesterol or triglycerides on the side of the fats, along with proteins. Note that the fats are called lipids, hence the name lipoproteins. Cholesterol as explained above is a waxy substance important in cell production.

Triglycerides are a type of fat that's produced by the liver or in the intestinal tract. It's used by the body to provide a reliable form of energy between meals. The triglycerides are stored in the cells of the body and when the body needs energy, its cells release the stored triglycerides into your bloodstream so that you can burn them up as an energy source. Your body produces enough triglycerides to sustain your energy in general scenarios. When you eat certain things, it can cause your liver and intestines to produce too many triglycerides, which can put your body at risk.

Low-density lipoproteins are also known as "bad

cholesterol." This is a type of lipid that leaves fatty plaque against the walls of your blood vessels. It constricts blood flow, thereby creating a risk of heart issues, such as coronary artery disease, strokes, and heart attacks. The condition of constricted vessels causing reduced blood flow is known as atherosclerosis.

Conventional medicines are used to bring down low-density lipoproteins with the purpose to lower heart-related risks. Statins are one category of medicine that's used, with non-pharmaceutical remedies including a healthy diet, ensuring your weight is in a healthy range, being active, exercising, and not smoking. Herbal medicine is an excellent source of combatting low-density lipoproteins. Some examples of herbs that can be used are basil and fenugreek leaves. Several spices and foodstuffs can be used to assist in lowering your low-density lipoprotein levels.

Having looked at some of the conditions that herbs can assist with, we'll now look at some well-known herbs that have many positive qualities.

CHAPTER 3

NATIVE AMERICAN WIDELY USED MEDICINAL PLANTS

This chapter contains the go-to herbs and plants used in Native American healing. Many others can be sought out for specific issues. This chapter is focused on the garden variety and the conditions that they can assist in healing.

Ginger of the Wild

Wild ginger is an incredibly versatile healer. It works wonders on the gastrointestinal tract, helping with flatulence, an upset stomach, ailments of the intestines, stomach aches, cramps, and indigestion. It helps with heart palpitations and other chest issues. You can use it chopped up and in a poultice for skin care and caring for open wounds. This is because wild ginger has antibiotic effects that kill fungi and bacteria. by taking it as tea, you can break a fever by inducing sweating, you can increase your appetite, you can use it for contraceptive purposes, and it can be used as a general tonic that gives your body a boost.

Lavender

Lavender has a host of medicinal benefits. It's good for the heart and blood-related conditions, acting to lower blood pressure and heart rate. Inhaling it as an essential oil is one of the recommended ways of using lavender for heart conditions, particularly if you're recovering from a heart operation. You can also use it for lung conditions. It works to alleviate asthma, mucus hyperplasia (having mucus cells where you're not supposed to have them), and reduce lung inflammation due to allergies. It's good for improving the quality of your sleep, whether you inhale the essential oil or drink the tea. Taking the tea is also useful for managing menopausal hot flashes.

Its antifungal content is good for athlete's foot, and ringworm. Despite being good for killing fungi, lavender is good for managing healthy levels of candida albicans (a yeast that's part of your healthy intestinal flora). Linalyl acetate and linalool are both compounds that are commonly found in lavender. They reduce pain and have anti-inflammatory effects, making them good for manual workers with muscle and joint pain. External applications for which lavender can be used are eczema, acne, inflammation of the skin, blemishes, and potentially with hair growth (clinical studies have shown it increases the number of hair follicles in mice).

Desert Lavender

Native American cultural groups often referred to desert lavender (also known as lavender bushmint) as lavender. It's an unrelated plant that grows in the form of a flowering shrub with some characteristics of lavender. The medicinal uses of desert lavender are gone into more detail here. The scientific name for this plant is hyptis emoryi.

Desert lavender is good for bleeding issues. It stems the flow of blood and is particularly effective for heavy menstrual bleeding. Other female inflammation is also positively affected by taking this herb (such as inflammation of the body due to hormones). This herb increases the energy in various body parts, thereby inducing body stabilization. When applied to the skin, this herb has a soothing effect on rashes, insect bites, scrapes, burns, and cuts. It can also be used to counter the inflammation of the skin and fungal infections growing on the skin.

As a tea, it's good for combating autoimmune dysfunctions, recovering from hangovers and using drugs, reducing chemical sensitivity (reacting excessively to normal levels of chemicals that others would be able to tolerate), and it's good for liver health. A tincture of desert lavender helps with upper GI tract inflammatory conditions, such as acid reflux, ulcers in the stomach or intestines, and hyper secretions of the stomach (making too much stomach acid).

Anxiety, tension, and stress can all be countered by taking desert lavender. It also helps with grounding and centering yourself, especially when breathed in as an essential oil. Insomnia can also be eased by taking this herb. Possibly the best part about these mental, nervous, and sleep-related conditions is that you can take the herb during the day without inducing sleepiness. You can even take it before driving without concern about being lulled to sleep.

Desert lavender contains monoterpenes, a substance used in metabolism and responsible for the plant's smell. This causes reduced tension in blood vessel walls, a lowered heart rate, and reduced blood pressure. It further contains sesquiterpenoids, a substance also contributing to the plant's smell. Sesquiterpenoids are good for cardiovascular diseases and are potentially anti-cancerous.

Honeysuckle

The scientific name for American honeysuckles is lonicera canadensis. It's used as a diuretic (i.e. for improved passing of urine). The stem covering is particularly good for urinary diseases. You can also use this herb as a blood purifier and as a natural sedative for children.

Chamomile

Most of us know about chamomile because of the commercialized use of its tea for calming your body and making you sleep better. It does have a host of other benefits as well. You can use chamomile for other nervous conditions, such as anxiety, depression, restlessness, and mental or emotional aspects that contribute to anorexia. It's good for your digestive system by assisting with indigestion, diarrhea, constipation, flatulence, ulcers in your digestive tract, and colic.

Asthma and bronchitis are two lung conditions that are affected positively by the use of chamomile. Gout and nerve pain (neuralgia) are both positively impacted by taking the herb, especially when applied externally. Other external benefits are reduction of hemorrhoids, soothing burns, assisting with healing wounds, counteracting nappy rashes, decreasing eczema, easing skin irritation, and subduing poison ivy reactions. You can also use it as a rub to help with oral health. Use it for gum bleeding, soreness of your gums, and baby teething pains or convulsions. Your eyes can also benefit from external application of the herb, specifically by counteracting pink eye and blocked tear ducts.

The herb is also good for concerns relating specifically to women. This includes painful menstruation and abnormal lack of menstruation. Breast infections and inflammation can be subdued with the herb, while cracked nipples can be soothed and healed by applying the herb.

Other conditions that can be positively affected by using chamomile are nasal conditions, ear infections, motion sickness, alcohol withdrawal, malaria, and chicken pox. Thus, it's a truly versatile herb.

Pineappleweed

Pineappleweed is sometimes referred to as chamomile by Native American tribes. It is a popular herb for medicinal remedies, scientifically known as Matricaria discoidea. It strengthens the immune system, which helps with fevers (by inducing sweating), parasitic infections, and parasitic infections such as intestinal worms. Nervous conditions such as stress, anxiety, and depression can be better by taking the herb. It makes an emotionally therapeutic sedative that helps to balance your mood—which in turn also makes it an effective agent against insomnia.

You can use pineappleweed to improve the condition of your skin. It's good for wrinkles, psoriasis, insect bites, and skin irritation. When used as a compress, it can help with pain (whether joint pain, chronic pain, or acute pain) by numbing the area it's applied to. When you get a wound, you can use this plant to prevent infection of the wound, heal the wound faster, and reduce pain in the wounded area.

It's great for digestive issues and conditions. It balances your intestinal flora. It further aids with an upset stomach, indigestion, constipation, bloating, and cramping. Other conditions pinappleweed are effective for are low milk production (only take it while breastfeeding, not while pregnant) and releasing toxins from your body.

Garlic

Garlic helps with shortness of breath and asthma by releasing mucus and phlegm from your lungs. Low vitamin C (i.e. scurvy) is remediable with garlic. It's also good for releasing gas and improving digestion. One last condition garlic is well-known for improving is high blood pressure.

Feverfew

Feverfew is aptly named considering that it's effective for

overcoming fevers. It's also a great herb to take to make headaches go away. It's also good for pain related to arthritis and toothaches. Malaria is a condition that has been overcome with the use of this herb. Further, it makes a good antiseptic, which helps a lot with wound care and the presence of unwanted microorganisms in your body. On a practical (albeit non-medicinal) note, feverfew can be used to repel insects and critters.

Ginger

Ginger root is mainly used for digestive conditions. It helps with gassiness, upset stomachs, stomach aches, cramps, indigestion, colic, and with increasing your appetite. You can also use it for heart palpitations and complaints in the chest region. When you have a fever, you can use ginger to induce sweating and break the fever—this is further assisted by the herb's antibiotic qualities. It has also been known to make a good contraceptive. General vigor can also be induced by using it as a tonic. As for external applications, it's good for healing open wounds and reducing skin inflammation.

Goldenseal

Goldenseal has multiple surface applications. It can be used in ointments to reduce eye inflammation. It is used as a rub for sore gums or oral ulcers. You can also use it on skin disorders and rashes. Digestive conditions, such as diarrhea, constipation, and an upset stomach can be remedied with goldenseal. Conditions such as fevers, colds, hay fever, and respiratory tract infections can also be cured with this herb.

Ginseng

Ginseng is a popular herb in the international community for its quality as a 'panacea' (a general cure-all). Some of the conditions it's great at overcoming are respiratory disorders, fevers, digestive issues, and excessive bleeding. You can use it to remedy pain too, whether taking it internally or applying it externally. Besides its ability to give you energy and vigor generally, ginseng more specifically gives the same qualities in the bedroom, making it a good aphrodisiac.

The Rose of the Wild

Wild rose is believed to do more than just heal physical and mental conditions. It's believed to be an aid for spiritual conditions as well. Native American communities use it to ward off harmful ghosts. It's also used by mourners when they're sleeping to ward off any spiritual entities that might be haunting them after a person close to them has passed away. As much as it's valuable for use with the dead, it's also useful for those entering a new life. It's used to give vitality to infants so that they survive and remain vital to adulthood.

Used externally, it can reduce spasming and inflammation, and it can make your skin more taught by reducing pore size. Used internally, it can be used to relax your liver as well as your nerves. More generally, it boosts your immune system and makes a good antiseptic. It's also a good aphrodisiac.

On a specific note, wild rose is a good herb for blood conditions. It's a blood mover (meaning it makes blood flow better through your blood vessels). As such, it prevents vascular congestion (too much blood in a group of blood vessels), hypertension, and unpredictable clotting. Predictable clotting makes this herb good for preventing excess bleeding from wounds. Wild rose is thus of general benefit to your heart. Further, it provides your heart with the nutrients it needs, ensuring your heart functions at optimal level.

Cactus of The Prickly Pear

The prickly pear is intensely soothing. When applied

externally, it can alleviate burns, reduce boils, and lighten scar tissues (especially scarring from TB). It can be applied to wounds for both antiseptic and blood stemming qualities. You can apply it to your genitals to help with urinary tract infections because it has antibiotic and antibacterial qualities.

Consuming the cactus and the fruit is good for sugar and blood-related conditions. The cactus reduces sugar absorption, blood sugar, and absorption of simple carbohydrates. As such, it's effective for assisting with weight loss and diabetes (particularly by curbing insulin shock). Further, the plant lowers cholesterol and assists with the prevention of cardiovascular diseases. And on an unrelated note, it's very good for managing a swollen prostate.

Mullein

Mullein is not Native to North America but has been used by Native Americans since it was brought over by Europeans. It's typically used for pain, particularly with rheumatism, teething, and cuts. It's also good for respiratory ailments, particularly the prevention of coughing.

Ashwagandha

This herb has been used extensively for nervous system conditions. It's good for coping with trees, improving your mood, and helping with a feeling of general wellness. You can take it to improve sleep as well. Pain can be alleviated with the herb, especially from headaches and menstrual cramps. You can apply it for the reduction of inflammation as well. A final set of issues that the herb is especially good for is improving your digestive system's functioning so that you don't face many digestive problems.

Licorice

Licorice isn't only tasty as a treat, but also effective as a healing agent. You can chew on it to relieve a toothache. You can chew on it or drink tea made from it to reduce coughing, chest pain, and a sore throat. Native American tribes have used it to strengthen the throat for singing purposes. It's also good for your oral health by relieving earache and combatting ear infections. You can use it to improve your digestive functions, thereby preventing diarrhea, upset stomach, and stomach aches. Finally, you can take the herb to assist in breaking fevers.

Hummingbird Blossom

The use of this plant and its flowers is multifarious. It's good for mouth and throat conditions. It helps with inflammation, burns, sores, and wounds. It stimulates the functioning of your kidney. You can use it to drain out blockages in your lymph system. It's uniquely effective at attacking fibroid tumors. And it can be used to bring down your blood pressure.

The Elm Slippery

Slippery elm is a tree that's used for surface conditions, respiratory problems, and issues relating to the digestive tract. On the surface, it can be used as a healing salve for wounds, skin inflammation, psoriasis, boils, and ulcers in your mouth. Respiratory problems you can handle with the tree include a sore throat and a lack of mucus production. Digestive issues you can handle with slippery elm are acid reflux, painful intestines, too much acid in the gastrointestinal tract, ulcers in the gastrointestinal tract, and diarrhea.

Willow

Willow trees have a host of benefits when used as herbal medicine. It can be used to staunch bleeding and to prevent dysentery (diarrhea mixed with blood and mucus). It can be used as a laxative—even for chronic diarrhea—as well as for constipation by both hydrating and adding mass to digested content. Further, it can help hydrate your body and prevent water retention.

Parasitic conditions like worms can be curbed with willow. So can sexually transmitted diseases such as gonorrhea. The use of this tree extends to the prevention of pain, whether the pain is internal or external. Further, it can be used to break a fever and overcome headaches. It's a panacea that is particularly useful for improving the speed of recovery after a disease. On an aesthetic note, you can use willow on your head to reduce dandruff. It also holds a spiritual significance, assisting with the departure of the spirits of the dead.

Yew

Yew has been used extensively for external applications. It can be used to cure skin diseases and the bark has in multiple cases helped people overcome skin cancer. When applied to the skin, yew protects against sunburn. You can also apply it to wounds so that they heal well. You can also use it for pain. Arthritis, rheumatism, internal injury and pain, headaches, and stomach aches are all pains that can be taken care of with this tree.

Your lungs can be strengthened using yew, alleviating conditions such as TB and bronchitis—particularly when made into a decoction. It can aid with stomach problems by improving the functioning of the digestive tract and curing ulcers. When you have a fever, you can use this tree to break the fever, particularly if you use it in a hot bath to induce sweating. Kidney and liver problems can also be alleviated with yew. Further, it can be taken by pregnant women to prevent them from going into labor, and an infusion of the leaves can be used by non-pregnant women to improve menstruation.

Yew is also known as a tonic, resulting in increased energy.

It can also increase strength and reduce dizziness.

The Thistle of Milk

Milk thistle is an effective herb for liver disorders such as hepatitis, cirrhosis, and jaundice. Gallbladder problems are also circumvented with this herb. Further, you can use it to manage diabetes better and to improve digestive functions.

Uva Ursi

Uva ursi is a very popular herb. It's good for urinary tract infections and keeping bacterial content in your urine. It's been used by both Native Americans and early European settlers of North America for this purpose. In places like Russia, the herb is used as a weight loss aid. Widespread uses for the herb include overcoming infections, shrinking your pores, and soothing the body.

CHAPTER 4

NATIVE AMERICAN PLANTS PROFILE

The previous chapter covered some of the benefits obtainable from commonly used herbs and plants. It focused on how Native American societies used and currently use these herbs to help members of this community. This chapter will focus on some useful herbs used in Native American healing.

Frangula Californica

This shrub is commonly found in the west of North America and is easily distinguished by its red or blackish berries. The seeds inside of the fruit are shaped like coffee beans, giving rise to the plant's nickname as the coffeeberry. The leaves can be made into a tea with a laxative effect. The tea is also used to overcome the flu and to boost kidney health. A decoction can be made of the leaves and mixed into ointments to dull pain from poison oak rashes and to keep infected wounds healthy. Make a mouthwash by steeping the roots in hot water and leaving it to cool; this is great for a toothache.

Hydrangea Cinerea

Also known as the ashy hydrangea, this bush has three or four-petaled flowers, as well as clusters of very small pollen-bearing flowers. The bottom of the leaves is covered in small gray hairs, which is what gives the plant the 'ashy' in its common name. This herb is mainly used as a laxative—by making a root infusion—and to induce vomiting (by making tea from the surface of the stem).

Ipomopsis Longiflora

You will find these small shrubs with lavender or white-colored flowers in the dry plains of the U.S. and Mexico. It's used by several tribes but holds particular importance to the Zuni people of New Mexico. The herb is chiefly used for eye health, being used as an eyewash after making an infusion from its leaves. Other names the herb is commonly known by are pale flower gilia, flaxflowered ipomopsis, and pale trumpets.

Labrador Tea

Labrador tea is a group of three rhododendron shrubs. The three species are R. groenlandicum (bog labrador tea), R. tomentosum (marsh labrador tea), and R. columbianum (western labrador tea). All three species are used to make medicinal tea, but it's suggested that only R. groenlandicum is used for this purpose because the other two can have toxic effects. The tea is very good for your respiratory tract—clearing away coughing, reducing congestion in your lungs, easing lung infections, and soothing sore throats. It's also popularly used as a rheumatism pain remedy, easing the soreness when drunk regularly.

Nicotiana Clevelandii

This plant is commonly called Cleveland's tobacco or wild tobacco. It's a small shrub found in western Mexico and the southwestern U.S. It's both smoked and used in other forms of herbal preparation. There's a spiritual connection with this plant in the Cahuilla tribe because it believed that it was one of the first plants that were created and that the sun was created to light tobacco that a god wanted to smoke. For medicinal uses, it can be made into a decoction. Avoid handling the leaves directly with your hands, particularly when the leaves are wet. The decoction is useful to take when you need to puke something up. Applied externally, the decoction is a good wash for cuts, bruises, swelling, and wounds.

Phlox Subulata

This plant is well-known for its appearance as a small bush with bright purple flowers. The common English name is moss phlox. The bush is particularly common in the eastern parts of the U.S. and Canada. You can use this plant to reduce pain you may feel, especially when applied topically. Other topical uses include using it as an eye was, counteracting eczema, and making boils go away. It's also particularly good for stomach ailments when taken orally. Most of the uses are brought about with a hot infusion (either using it as a wash for the body or drinking it as a tea).

Salix Exigua

Also called the coyote willow or sandbar willow, this is a species of tree or shrub in the willow family. It has white and yellow catkins and lance-shaped leaves. The plant's medicinal uses are rather wide. It can be used to alleviate toothache, to overcome venereal diseases, stomach issues, wound care, and dandruff. It contains a chemical that has a similar effect to aspirin, making this plant good for pain. You can make a tea by drying out the bark, steeping it in hot water, and then straining out the bark pieces. The tea is very good for pain management.

With an understanding of the profile of some particularly useful North American medicinal plants, we're now going to look at how to effectively source and extract them.

CHAPTER 5

SOURCING EXTRACTING OF HERBS

How and where you source your herbs plays a big part in the quality of the medicine you make with it. If you get your herbs from a good source and extract using reliable processes, you'll be able to provide your patients with the quality results they need. Making sure that you're getting the plants you need is the first step in creating a reliable assortment of natural healing remedies.

Collection

Collecting herbs is different from using homegrown herbs. You're taking herbs directly from the wild, resulting in herbs that contain most of their natural characteristics, including a full flavor profile. Proper herb collection can result in better herb growth into the future. You need to harvest at the correct time to ensure you have an optimal concentration of essential oils. This would be the right time of the year and the right time of the day.

The right time of the year is before the plant gets too old because old specimens lose intensity of their essential oils, their flavors, and other qualities. Just before, or at the time they start blooming is the optimal time of year to harvest flowering plants. The right time of the day is early in the day before the sun has evaporated the oil and nutrient concentrations of the plant. In the morning when the dew's just evaporated is a great time to harvest.

There are a few methods you can use to perform a harvest. Using your fingers is great for harvesting leaves and small twigs of most herbs. Woody herbs will require scissors or snips because using your fingers will just break the stem and damage the plant. Use of pruners results in clean cuts that allow the herb to perform further growth. Cutting at the base of the main stem (i.e. ground emergence) allows for future growth. Breaking off buds encourages future leaf growth. Cutting or breaking off the flower where it emerges from the stalk is good for future growth. While it's best to collect seeds by snipping or breaking them off at their base.

Natural Drying

The simplest method of drying herbs is using natural drying. This is an ancient technique that still produces reliable results today. It will yield quality results and works practically everywhere except for the most humid of climates. The process starts by cleaning the stems that have been harvested, then letting them dry out. This is followed by removing imperfect specimens (such as ones that look infected) from the rest of the bunch.

Bundle the healthy stems together and hang them upside-down in a dry, warm space. The space needs air exposure and mustn't be directly exposed to the sun. Leave them to hang until they dry (which could take anywhere between a few days and a few weeks). You'll know it's dry when the leaves crumble between your fingers. Some people like keeping the stems and leaves whole, while others like crumbling them into bits. Both preferences can work for medicinal uses.

Processing

Processing is when you put the herbs through steps to optimize their medicinal use. Different processes depending on how you want to use the herb. The part of the herb used also affects the processing, for example, bark will be processed differently than flowers. Bark is rough and tough, while flowers are dainty and delicate, necessitating processing techniques that preserve the integrity of both plant parts.

Processing Equipment

Machines are normally specialized to an industrial level. They might be made by mechanical engineers that take clients' exact needs into account. If making a juice, for example, the client will need some sort of press with a filter. If using it as a dried powder in capsules, the herb will need to be crushed/pummeled, then ground, then sifted. Typical industrial equipment includes dryers, dehydrators, cutting machines, threshers (separates seeds or grains from crops), classifiers that use air to blow lighter parts of the plant into one container while other parts remain behind, mixers (for different types of herbs), and blenders to chop up and make plants fine. Machines used to process herbs on a household level include dehydrators, an oven, a blender for making pastes, pots to make teas and washes, and a double boiler to make essential oil.

Crushing/Chopping

You can crush fresh and dry herbs, both with different purposes. Crushed dried herbs are used for consumption and for mixing into creams or other mixtures. Fresh herbs are crushed to form compresses, pastes, or to supplement meals. Fine chopping is done with fresh herbs with the purpose of adding the herbs to food or to release the juices for you to rub the herb directly onto your skin. Rougher chopping is done to make material for tea.

Destemming

Destemming involves removing leaves from a stem. The

stem isn't always wanted, especially when it's hard or woody. It might have nutrients and medicinal qualities, but normally we focus on the medicinal qualities of the leaves. You can pluck off leaves one by one, or to make things faster a cheese grater is a grate option. Pull the stem through a large hole in the grater. The leaves will be pulled off while the stem is pulled out the other side. You can use similar things that have a hole with the right size to make the process speedy.

Screening

A screen is an alternative tool for the natural drying process. It is a frame with mesh or a net stretched between it. The mesh supports flowers and other plant parts. It's got good exposure to air all around it. Further, you can use a screen on delicate herbs and delicate plant parts that can't be tied into bunches for hanging. You can even make stackable screening frames, which allows for multiple herbs to be dried at the same time.

Quality Control

Quality control makes sure that you don't end up with useless herbs and herbal products. Nothing dampens the spirit like lack of results. Low quality herbs give a lack of results in the healing department. This section lists some ways you can ensure that you get herbs that give the results you're looking for.

Document Verification

Documentation is important when importing herbs. It shows what the grade of the herb is (medicinal, food, or otherwise). It also shows if it's high quality medicinal or average quality. There might be chemicals in some where there aren't chemicals in others of the same species due to growing conditions—which would be listed in the documentation.

When buying herbs from overseas or from industrial herbal suppliers it's important to make sure that you're getting what you ordered. First look at the label on the container. It will show you when there are unexpected additions in the supplement (for example, heavy metals). You might need to clear up some terms to understand the label fully.

When you're getting herbs from a source that provides a chemical analysis, you should look it over. Look out for any heavy metals, toxic substances as these aren't good for you. Specific things you want to look out for are arsenic; radioactive contamination; aflatoxins (toxic compounds produced by certain molds that can damage your liver and are carcinogenic); microbes, yeasts, and molds (showing lack of hygiene and contamination); and residue of pesticides.

Visual Control

Look at the herbs you've obtained. You'll see when there are indications that it's not in optimal condition. There are signs such as blotchiness or discoloration when you've obtained herbs of non-optimal quality. Also, look out for mold or fungi. Be vigilant for things mixed in with your herb that shouldn't be there. One such instance is when more than one herb or plant is mixed together. You'll see that there's something in with the herb you ordered that shouldn't be there

Wrong color, a mix of colors, and things that shouldn't be mixed in, like bug parts or sand are all red flags. You can use different types of light and meters if you have them. This will allow you to spot contaminants of various sorts.

Analytical Control

Analytical techniques determine the constituent compounds in the herb. Various techniques and tests used to determine whether the necessary biological components for medical value are present. The tests also determine when there are things in the herb that shouldn't be there. A thermal test (inducing heat and seeing what the results are) can test the absolute water content and the crystal water content, interactions between components in the herb or in a herbal drug, and stability of substances in a herb.

Chromatography is the practice of placing things in a substance and determining qualities about them based on the variations of movements of the content being analyzed (i.e. some moving slower or faster or spreading out more). HPTLC (high-performance thin-layer chromatography) performs qualitative and quantitative measures that can be compared. Marker compound identity (the active ingredients that determine the identity of a particular herb or medicine) and percentage of purity can both be tested with HPTLC. Analysis is done on a sample and it's both accurate and simple.

The above are but two of many measures that can be taken to analyze the content of a herbal medicine or the quality of a herb. Contact a lab if you want to get a full analysis done. When you're using your home-grown herbs to make your medicines or harvesting herbs from the wild, the above won't be necessary unless you're going to go into commercial herbalism.

Extraction Methods

Extrication methods are used to get the active ingredients out of a herb. As a result, you can get concentrated forms of herbs. There are multiple extrication methods. This section will give you a comprehensive review on the subject. In extraction, the medically active components are dissolved; the inert components remain solid.

Factors to Be Considered in Choosing Extraction Method

Do you have the right equipment? If you don't, can you and are you willing to buy it? If you can't, are you able to build the equipment you need to the standard you need within your budget? Do you have the materials you need to perform that type of extraction? This process of elimination will get you to the types of extraction that are feasible to you.

What is the intended purpose of extraction? Do you want stronger medicinal usages, or do you want slightly weaker uses that you can continue using over protracted periods of time? For example, you wouldn't extract the essential oils of a plant if you want a daily tonic. For a daily tonic you would probably dry out the herb and then make a tea (i.e. a hot infusion) from it daily.

Forms of Extraction

Solvent extraction is the most common. First, the selected solvent penetrates the solid matrix. Then the solute dissolves the solvent. The solute is then diffused out of the solid matrix. The extracted solutes are collected. The selection of the solvent is crucial for solvent extraction. Selectivity, solubility, cost, and safety should all be considered in selection of solvents.

The distillation method is purification of a liquid by evaporating it and then cooling it. Hydro distillation is one way, while steam distillation is another. Both are very good at extracting oils out of the plant. Steam distillation is used more commonly than hydro distillation. This extraction method is mainly used to get essential oil out of the herb. Essential oils are probably the most concentrated form of herbal medicine and normally need to be diluted for medicinal consumption.

Pressing as a form of extraction gives an output that's

almost like a juice of the herb. You need to use fresh herbs and can't use dried herbs. You use a piece of equipment called a tincture press, which is normally an expensive piece of equipment. Alternatives that don't work as well are apple presses and potato ricers. Normally for larger-scale herbal medicine production, the press squeezes out the liquids and leaves behind a dry pulp. The liquid is squeezed through perforated and filtering tools to remove impurities or solid bits.

Stability to Heat

You need to be able to maintain the heat of your apparatus or in the process to get your intended results. When you're making a decoction, you need to maintain the summer so that the leaves' content is drawn out effectively. When you're making a cold infusion, you don't want to forget it in the sun and then have a mushy, rotten mush. Thus, you need to be able to maintain the relevant temperature needed over the time period you require it.

Nature of Solvent

Solvents work by dissolving a substance or a part of a substance. The result is a mixture between the solvent and the mixed substance. The most commonly used solvents are water, alcohol, and oils. These solvents can be consumed by humans, thus allowing the substances that have been dissolved into them to enter the human body at the same time. The molecules of the herb that have been extracted into the solvent are normally evenly dispersed through the mixture when done right. In some cases, the solvent may be evaporated, leaving behind only the biochemical residue (although this isn't normally done in traditional herbalism).

Cost of the Drug

When you're making herbal drugs for your own practice or

for the health of your community, you won't usually have large financial resources at your disposal at first. As such, you'll need to use a form of extraction that suits your budget. Some forms of extraction can cost thousands of dollars to establish (specifically when you take the cost of the equipment into consideration). The more complex the method, the more time you'll have to dedicate to learning how to extract it with that method (time being another cost).

Then there's the consideration of running costs. If you're making tinctures using alcohol that you bought at your local drug store, it would be inhibitive for you to charge low prices to your patients. If you get wholesale costs and it doesn't cost much, then you can charge less to make a profit. This makes your healthcare more accessible to those in your community. The costs of extracting your herbs are thus relevant to your selection of extraction methods.

Duration of Extraction

Sometimes extraction can take a long time. Tinctures are an example of this because they take between six and eight weeks to make. This differs from something such as percolation, which can be used to extract a herb in a matter of hours. Depending on when you need the herbs, you'll alter your decision as to which form of extraction you're going to use. Being prepared for the patients you see requires that they don't spend weeks waiting for the appropriate medicine they need.

Intended Use

The intended use of the herbal medicine will be a valid consideration when selecting your extraction. If you're going to use it for topical applications, then you want something that will be able to mix well into an ointment or cream. If you're going to be using it for internal consumption, then it must be safe to consume. Essential oils, for example, are too strong for direct consumption. Essential oils need to be diluted into carrier oils in order to be safe for ingestion or for mixing in with a cream or ointment.

Commonly Used Methods in the Extraction of Medicinal Plants

Select from the following forms of extraction for good medicinal herb uses. There are differences to these techniques when making herbal medicine on a large scale or a clinical scale. But, for traditional use as a herbalist, this section contains the usual steps to follow for each method.

Maceration

This consists of extracting herbal qualities into oil. It can be used for skincare and external applications. You start with having the right oil for your purpose. Don't use one you're allergic to or which your patients are allergic to. Have the dried herb that you want to macerate, taking a moment to break up the herb finely. Then get an airtight container. Put the herb into the container, followed by pouring over oil (until it's covering the herb). Put the jar in a warm, sunny location for up to three weeks, removing the herbs from the oil and putting in new herbs after the three-week period.

Alternatively, use a bain-marie or double boiler. Put in the herbs and cover them with oil. Keep it in there for an hour when using a double boiler or bain-marie. You can also use a slow cooker. If you use a slow cooker, put in the herbs and cover them with oil. Then leave it on a low heat overnight. Strain out the herb bits so that you're only left with oil. Put into airtight containers—small containers are better because smaller amounts are exposed to air at a time. When not exposed to air, deterioration takes place more slowly. Macerated oil normally keeps from six to twelve months.

Including a small amount of vitamin E oil will keep the oils from going rancid too fast. About 1% of your mixture should be vitamin E oil. You know it's rancid when it starts smelling funny after a few months.

Infusion

Hot herbal infusions are also known as tea. This method draws out vitamins, enzymes, and aromatic volatile oils. Steep time will depend on your personal flavor preferences and the specific herbs used. Longer steeping leads to stronger flavors. Steep herbal teas for longer than you would with usual teas you buy in the grocery store. The steps start with putting a desired amount of fresh or dried herb in your mug or teapot (normally one to three tablespoons if you use a teapot). Pour over boiling water and let it steep. Steeping between 15 minutes and an hour will give you the desired results.

Cold herbal infusions can be made with almost all herbs. Mucilaginous herbs are best extracted with a cold infusion. It's also really good with freshly harvested herbs that you don't plan on drying. It lasts a week or less, so get rid of it if it starts smelling odd. The steps start with filling a jar with cold water (a quart jar is commonly used). Bundle an ounce of the herb into a cheesecloth, then submerge the bundle. Screw on the cap and leave it to infuse over the course of the day or overnight. You can also put the herbs into the water and just strain it after it's overnighted.

Decoction

This is a hot extraction similar to tea. You boil the herb in a pot of water. The process is good for extracting from tougher materials like veiny stems and roots. It's stronger and more concentrated than infusions. The steps are to put three tablespoons of the herb in a small saucepan filled with a quart of water. Heat it to a simmer, then cover it. Simmer for 20 to

45 minutes, followed by straining the liquid into a quart jar. It lasts for up to a week in the refrigerator. Alternatively, you can freeze it into ice cubes or popsicles which you can eat as is, or melt into foods and juices.

Percolation

Normally alcohol or water is used as the solvent when percolating. You move the solvent through a powdered herb very slowly. The solvent then drips into a container beneath the percolator—with a very strong liquid resulting. It's a process that can take anywhere from a few hours up to two days. You need either a percolator or an alternative piece of equipment (a homemade percolator). There are multiple websites with easy DIY steps to make your own percolator.

The steps are to moisten 100 grams of powder with some of the solvent so it looks grainy, then leave it for 12 to 24 hours to hydrate (the rehydrated powder will be slightly expanded). Put the moistened powder into the percolator cone, followed by pouring in 500 milliliters of your chosen solvent—either water or alcohol. The solvent will go through the herbal material and drip out the cone's tap over a few hours.

Tincture

You'll need alcohol of a high proof—80 or more for normal plant matter, and 180 for non-water-soluble herbal parts— 180 proof for herbs with no water-soluble parts. Vodka is commonly used, while whiskey is also used with some herbs. You can also use strong vinegar. Tinctures are effective because alcohol extracts components of the herb that water wouldn't be able to extract.

The steps are to gather the parts of the herb you're going to extract from (dry or wet). Any toxic parts of the herb should be excluded. Put the herbs into an airtight container, then cover it with the alcohol. Fresh herbs should have a 1:1 ratio with the alcohol. Dried herb should have a 1:4 ratio with the alcohol. This is followed by sealing the jar. Place it out of direct sunlight and leave it there for six to eight weeks. Shake it every few days to make sure that content is continually extracted from all the herbal parts in the jar. Strain the resulting liquid into small dark glass jars. Label it with some basic information (date of creation being one). Tinctures last about 10 years.

Essential Oil

Essential oils are the oils that give a herb its flavor or scent. They are captured as oils that can evaporate easily (i.e. volatile oils). They are strong and contain many of the biologically active materials in the herb. You use essential oils in healing practices such as aromatherapy. They are considered to be a pure form of the medicine (i.e. its essence), because anything extracted using alcohol or other chemicals is automatically disqualified from being called an essential oil. It only qualifies if it's been extracted using evaporation techniques with water, or cold press techniques that apply a lot of pressure on the herb to squeeze out the oil.

The steps start with collecting the herb you would like to make into an essential oil. It should be fresh because you want to capture the oils, and dried herbs don't contain much oil. Chop it up—finely—to best extract the oils. You can use multiple herbs if you want to create an essential oil blend. The process will require either a crockpot with a lid or a double boiler. This description will cover how to make essential oil using a crockpot.

Put in about three cups of your chopped herbs, then fill up your crockpot halfway with water (making sure you cover the herbs). Put the lid upside down on the crockpot. This will allow any oils that evaporate to condensate on the lid and drip back into the water. Heat up the water, then put it down to the lowest setting so that the water simmers for four hours. After four hours have passed, switch off the crockpot and leave the mixture to cool down for a few hours.

Once it's cooled, place it in the fridge overnight so that any essential oils in the water have a chance to congeal on the top of the water. The congealed film can be removed from the crockpot the next morning and placed into dark glass bottles. The film is the essential oil and will melt once it's at room temperature. You'll need to be fast so that it doesn't melt before you've managed to put it into the glass containers. Close the glass bottles and label them. The label normally includes a description of the herbs used and the date it was bottled. It should last about ten years before expiring.

Glycerite

You use vegetable glycerine (liquid vegetable fats and oils) to preserve with this method. It's an alternative to extracting with alcohol, which can be good for those who have personal beliefs that conflict with alcohol consumption or have an alcohol intolerance. You need the herb of your choice, which can be dried or fresh herbs. But, if you use dried herbs, you'll need to first rehydrate them. Rehydration is done by soaking the herb in some water, after which you can pour the glycerine into the herb-water mix. There should be about 70% glycerine to 30% water-herb mixture when you're using dried herbs.

When using fresh herbs, fill two-thirds of a mason jar with the herbs, then make a mixture of one quarter distilled water and two thirds glycerine and mix or shake it together. Pour in the water-glycerine mixture until the mason jar is full, then close the jar and store it out of direct sunlight for four to six weeks. Shake it daily during that time period. When the four to six-week period has passed, strain out the herbs and pour the glycerine into jars.

Once extracted, the glycerite-herb mixture will last between one and two years (if the glycerine was fresh when the extract was made). Make sure you label it so that you know when the glycerite was bottled so that you don't use it past its expiration date.

There are other methods to extract herbs, but those are generally reserved for industrial processes, rather than homemade processes. With knowledge about how to extract your herbs, the next chapter will show you how to harvest, store, and dry the herbs you need for extraction.

CHAPTER 6
HARVESTING, STORING, DRYING HERBS

You need to know how to get and keep your herbs so that you have enough stock for your medical practice. This chapter will describe how to harvest, store, and dry your herbs so that you can use them in your medicinal practice.

Harvesting Herbs

You can harvest herbs in any old way, or you can harvest them using methods that will keep the plant healthy for future harvests.

When to Harvest

To preserve medicinal qualities of herbs, make sure you harvest them at the right time. Harvest during the morning or very late in the day (morning being the better of the two options). Harvesting during the middle part of the day is worst because some of the oils will have evaporated, and because the plant will be wilted to some extent.

Also harvest the herb at the right time of the year. Many herbs can be harvested year-round, but some die over the winter and some should be harvested in their second year of growth for best results. Those that die down every year over the fall and winter periods should be harvested when their leaves are healthy and green during the spring and summer seasons. It's best to harvest them when the leaves are younger, but they can be harvested at any time.

Herbs that grow as biennials (plants that live for two years) normally grow a wreath of basal leaves in their first year. The wreath dies over the fall and winter months, after which the wreath, a flower stalk, and stalk leaves grow during the second year. Some of them can be harvested during both years, while with others it's better to harvest them during the first or second year (normally the second). Take this on a case by case basis by reading up on each herb's suggested harvesting period when you're planning on harvesting herbs of a particular kind.

Sustainable Harvesting

If you don't harvest your herbal supplies sustainably, then you'll lose the source of your medicine. The solution is to plant more of the herb if the demand is too great for the quantity of herbs that you're getting from your garden or plot of land. The same applies to herbs you harvest from foraging sources. If you use up too much of the available herb source at a foraging location, then you and others won't be able to get the stock they need. The solution in this case is to harvest what's sustainable at a particular site, and then find more of that herb to forage at a different site if you still need plant stock for your medicine.

Native Americans come from a heritage of living in unison with the environment. The cultures of the Americas respect the natural world and do what they can to prevent the natural environment from being destroyed. Harvesting in line with Native American heritage includes consideration of the flora and fauna as part and parcel of foraging trips. Since the environment provides the nourishment and the medicine that's needed to keep you and others healthy, it stands to reason that the environment should be given the chance to remain healthy itself. Destructive harvesting practices prevent this.

Another consideration is the weather. Plants that can be harvested the whole year around shouldn't be harvested too much during the colder months. Harvesting large quantities of a herb during colder months will prevent the herb from building itself up properly against the cold because the cold can make it difficult for new growth to come out. The cold also makes new growth slower, especially when the plant is living on energy and food reserves that it stored for use over the colder months in rhizomes or other food structures.

Leaves

Harvesting the leaves of a herb correctly ensures that you have the maximum amount of harvested material both at present and when harvesting in the future. By doing it properly, not only is the herb kept from permanent damage, but it's also motivated to produce leaves in larger quantities to cope with routine removal. Mint is an example of a plant that produces leaves in larger and larger quantities when it's plucked routinely.

With leaves that grow on annual plants, pinch off the leaves with the tips of your fingers at the tip of the stem. If the leaf is too tough to be gotten off in this way, snip it off with scissors or cutters. Perennial herbs (i.e. herbs that live for many years) are best harvested by cutting off stems of leaves. Do this by cutting off the stem at the base where it comes out of the ground or out of a branch. The stems will re-grow and will often branch into multiple stems.

Flowers

Flowers should be harvested when they're still buds or when they're starting to bloom. You can harvest them until the plant stops flowering, but when it reaches the point of maximum bloom (i.e. the majority of the flowers are in bloom), many of the flowers will start losing the essential oils and other bioactive ingredients they contain. The flower buds are often better for medical purposes than open flowers because the buds contain higher concentrations of natural oils and bioactive ingredients. Harvesting early in the day while it still has high water content is best. The result is minimal wilting of the flower. Use small snips for the best result so that the cut beneath the flower is clean. With herbs that live multiple years (especially if they flower all-year round), cutting flowers from the plant often will motivate the plant to produce more flowers. This can commonly be seen in herbs such as lavender.

Seeds

The main thing to keep in mind when harvesting seeds is the season when the herb you intend on harvesting goes into seed. For most plants this occurs in late summer or early fall. This could vary from species to species, so it's best to consult a field guide so that you don't miss the seed's harvest season. The seeds are collected in different ways, depending on the herb you're harvesting. For example, chia seed heads are easily harvested by shaking their seed heads into bags. This is the case with most herb seeds, although some might need to be plucked or removed in some other way.

Roots and Rhizomes

Many roots and rhizomes can be harvested without killing the herb plant. This is normally accomplished by removing the herb from the ground, cutting off a part of the root system or a part of the rhizome, then planting the herb again. Water it and make sure it's firmly secured in the ground. With some herbs the plant will die because of using the rhizome. In this case, it would be prudent to make sure that you're not taking the root of the only specimen present in a wild zone.

Roots should be harvested during late fall or early winter. At this point the herb has built up the food reserves it needs to get through the colder months, meaning the roots or rhizomes are at full capacity. It's best to do it when the plant has lost its leaves (if it loses leaves over the winter months). With biennials, it's best to harvest the root during the fall or winter of the first year. This is because it's collected nutrients the entire first year so that it would have enough energy to grow the flower stalk, to bloom, and to spread its seed.

Storing Herbs

Herb storage keeps your stock ready for use over long periods of time. When you don't make a concerted effort to preserve them for storage purposes, they'll go off faster. By making storage efforts, you can use the stock you have for long periods of time, even at medicinal quality. There have been many advances over the last few thousand years in the preservation of herbs, most of them being extremely easy and straightforward to use.

When storing herbs fresh, it's important to keep them cool and from overexposure to light and air. By keeping them cool, you're keeping the chemical breakdowns caused by heat from taking place. Keeping the herbs in a cool cupboard or in the fridge are two ways to keep it from getting too hot. Note that a fridge absorbs moisture out of the things that are stored in it. As such, your herbs will wilt unless you keep them in an airtight container if you use a fridge.

Keeping your herbs from light exposure prevents certain chemical reactions from taking place. As such, it's advantageous to keep the herbs away from windows or in cupboards. If you're storing them in airtight containers, it would be a good idea to use darkened containers that allow little light to come through. Airtight containers provide the added benefit of keeping the herb from being exposed to the air. Air contributes to the decomposition of plant matter, particularly when there are microbes involved, thus it's beneficial to keep the herbs from exposure.

Even with all the above steps followed for storage, fresh herbs won't last very long. Depending on the herb, they normally last about one to two weeks. Freezing the herbs will allow them to last much longer, as well as drying them. Both methods of preservation will be described below.

Freezing Herbs

Freezing is one of the most effective ways to make herbs and other plants last for long periods of time. Many of the medicinal qualities of a herb are conserved when you freeze it. There are multiple ways in which you can freeze herbs (which will be described in this section). The one piece of advice to heed when freezing as a form of preservation is that you shouldn't double freeze any herbs. The herbs will be slightly wilted and many cell walls will be broken because of freezing. When freezing it a second time, the cell wall destruction by ice crystals drops the quality far below required standards.

Ice Tray With Oil or Butter

Using an ice tray to preserve your herbs is a great way to get single portions of herbs for everyday use. You would use oil ice cube preservation for food purposes, more than medicinal purposes, but it will nevertheless provide a valuable source of nutrition to your diet. The great thing about preserving your herbs in this way is that you'll get the dose of herbs and the dose of oil you need to give your meals the punch of flavor they need. Drop it into your dish to add flavor to a sauce. Or, put it in your pan to give both flavor and grease to fry food. Alternatively, let it melt and use it in fresh dishes, such as salads (thereby making a tasty salad dressing).

The process to freeze herbs in this way is very simple. Simply chop your herbs finely, placing some of the chopped herb in each cube holder. Then pour over the oil of your choice. If you want to use butter instead, first melt it on a low heat so that you can pour the butter into each cube holder. Alternatively, put the herbs and oil or melted butter in a blender and whiz it into a puree. The puree can then be poured into the ice tray's cubes. When the tray is full, pop it in the freezer and allow it to freeze.

Ice Tray with Water

You can follow the same procedure as above, but using water instead of oil or butter. You could thus still use the herbs for cooking purposes, but you wouldn't alter the flavor of your food with the oil or butter of your choice. This could be useful when you're trying to impart a fresh flavor to a dish without imparting a sense of richness. You would generally put these ice cubes into dishes while you're cooking them because the freezing would have caused them to go limp, which would make it impractical to try and use it uncooked. Using water-herb cubes can be a good way to store herbs for some medicinal purposes too. You could store your herbs as ice cubes, and when you need to make a poultice or some similar healing tool, you could defrost the cube you need and mix it in with other ingredients.

You don't have to use conventional ice trays for preserving your chopped up herbs. If you want to use larger amounts at a time, nothing prevents you from making larger ice cubes using a container of a different size. As a practical tip, many people wait for the cubes to freeze, and then pop the frozen blocks into a ziploc packet for storage in the freezer, this protects the herbs better against freezer burn or some other undesirable situation (such as spilling cubes inside your freezer when trying to remove one for use).

Sealed Bags and Containers

Using a sealed bag is an easy way to store herbs—you simply chop up the herb and put it in small ziploc bags. Put in as much of the herb as you think you'll use at a time. Alternatively, you can use an airtight container for frozen herbs—this is particularly useful for herbs that can be kept on a stem. You put the herbs (still attached to their stem) on a tray in the freezer. Once the herbs are frozen, you transfer them into a sealable jar of some sort. Then when you need some of that herb, you simply remove one of the stems with leaves attached and use it for its intended purpose.

Drying Herbs

Drying herbs is a preferred method of herb preservation by many herbalists. You can use the herb for long periods after harvest when you've preserved them by drying. Drying herbs correctly will keep their flavor and will keep the majority of their healing qualities intact. Dried herbs are also incredibly versatile since they can be ground into powders for multiple uses (such as making capsules or for extraction of medicinal qualities into a liquid), or broken into smaller pieces to be used in anything ranging from teas to glycerides, or they can be kept whole for many of the same purposes.

What Herbs Can You Dry?

There are some herbs that are better fresh than dry (in terms of flavor), but all herbs can be dried and used to beneficial results. There are some that taste better dry than fresh, but once again, all herbs can be dried and used in ways that are beneficial to the user. You can make a list distinguishing what herbs taste better dried out and what herbs taste better fresh. But, if you do make such a list, note that you can still use all herbs beneficial if they've been dried, so the list would only be a matter of preference.

How to Store Dried Herbs?

Storing dried herbs is done in similar ways to storing fresh herbs. Use an airtight container for best results. The airtight container will prevent the herbs from going stale and from picking up microorganisms or chemically breaking down from exposure to air. Store the container in a dry location for best results, such as in a cupboard or in an opaque container that doesn't let light come in. Keeping the herbs in containers also prevents them from being exposed to humidity, which helps combat mold growth and the breakdown of the herb. Storing the herb in a container of sorts will also insulate it against temperatures that are too hot, especially if the container is kept in a cupboard, resulting in less chemical reactions that could break down the herb.

Keep a note of when the herbs were dried and stored. Herbs lose their flavor and go stale when they've been stored for long periods of time. This is even more the case when the herb container has been opened multiple times, thereby allowing new air in that breaks down the herb more each time the container is opened. An alternative that gets around this situation is to use vacuum packing or to use ziploc bags. When using these storage methods, you can store the amount of herbs you need and you can keep them unexposed to the elements.

To ensure the herbs keep their flavor and other qualities after being dried, it's best not to cut them up. Store them as close to the whole as you can, and then break, grind, or use the leaves you need as you need them. Also make sure they're dried out properly because if the herbs are slightly moist, mold and other bacteria can grow, and the herb will lose its beneficial values.

Drying Methods

There are a few ways to dry herbs. The best ones for the purpose of medicinal herb use are the traditional way and with a dehydrator. You can use an oven, but it's not as effective when you want to give it to patients for healing purposes. Below there's a brief description of these types of drying processes.

Oven Drying

The reason oven drying isn't the optimal process for medicinal herbs is that the nutrients and healthy components can break down to some extent. This is because when herbs are put in the oven, they cook a bit. Drying a herb in the oven requires that you first place all the herbs on a baking tray. The oven should then be preheated to a low temperature. The optimum temperature is about 180 degrees Fahrenheit.

Some people suggest having the oven open a bit, and others suggest having it closed. When you leave it open it allows any moisture that's evaporated from the herbs to leave the oven, which can make the process more effective. Leave the herbs in for about 4 hours, or until it crumbles when touched with an oven utensil. When it's at a crumbling point, it's easiest for the herb to be powdered and used in various forms of medication.

Dehydrating

A dehydrator works far better than an oven when you're making herbal medicine. It doesn't cook away the nutrients of the plant, leaving you with the qualities that you want to use in your medicines. When you've dehydrated them, you'll get a high quality result that you can use in multiple forms of medicine. Further, without any exposure to the elements, the herb remains pure and clean.

A tip to follow is to make sure that you don't stack herbs onto each other. They should be spread out in one layer. Or, if you have one with trays, one layer per tray. If you have layers piled on top of each other, you're not going to get consistent results. You would hate to provide medicines to patients that start molding because some of the content wasn't dried properly.

In terms of settings, you should use a low setting if you want quality results. Around 100 degrees Fahrenheit is best for most herbs. When you're in a humid region, then you can take it up to 125 degrees. Keep it in until you know it's fully dry. The amount of time it takes will depend on the model you're using, so check your dehydrator's manual for full information. A good way to confirm that it's ready is to feel it and see if it crumbles relatively easily to the touch.

Air Drying

The traditional method is very easy to use. It produces good quality medicinal herbs with no demand for any type of equipment. It might not work in very humid areas, like much of Florida, but it will work in areas with moderate to low humidity. If you live in a humid area, then a dehydrator is your best bet. The traditional drying technique is the method that's been used by cultures for thousands of years, and it hasn't failed them yet. By following their lead, you'll ensure that your traditional healing keeps with custom.

The process is simply to tie the herbs into bunches and then hang them up in the shade. They should be hung in an area that has a reasonable amount of airflow. It would also be beneficial if the spot where it's hung is hot (so long as the heat is dry and out of direct sunlight). The reason you don't want to have it in direct sunlight is because this will wash out the color and some of the beneficial qualities of the herb, which would defeat the purpose.

Once you've found an appropriate place to hang up your herb bunches, leave them there for about a week. You should feel when it's dry to the touch and it breaks easily between your fingers. At this point you can take it down and store it until you need it. Many herbalists would powder the herb at this point because powdered herbs are more compact and are easy to mix together and into medicinal media.

The takeaway of these drying methods is that there are high quality dried herbs and low quality dried herbs. Look at the product you intend on buying to see if the color is good. If you have the opportunity to taste it or smell it, you want to make sure that the scent and flavor come through strongly. This way you know it's not washed out and that it'll manage to produce potent effects on patients—or at least effects of the intended strength.

Microwave Drying

The main benefit when drying herbs using a microwave is that it's faster than the other methods. It's a straightforward process, only requiring your herbs, a paper towel, and a microwave. Spread the herbs out on the paper towel and put it in the microwave for 30 seconds. Flip the herbs, then pop them back in the microwave for a further 30 seconds. Repeat the flip and microwave process until the herbs are fully dried. It might be beneficial to reduce the microwave increments to 15 seconds at a time, especially when it comes to fragile and intricate herbs.

How to Cook With Dried Herbs

Use less dried herbs when cooking than cooking with fresh herbs. Cooking with fresh herbs requires about three times as much herb as cooking with its dried counterpart. Add them into your dishes and sauces while you're cooking. In this way, they'll have ample time to release their flavor into the dish. Saucy dishes are especially good for this purpose, particularly when they take at least a moderate amount of time to make. You can also flash fry the herbs with some butter and then drizzle it over a dish (such as a piece of steak) to give a strong bite of flavor to any dish.

This chapter covered how to get and how to keep your herbs for various uses. The next chapter will detail how to process the herb's you've obtained so that you can use them therapeutically.

CHAPTER 7
HERBAL PREPARATION AND DOSAGES

Preparing herbs for medicine makes use of multiple processes. These processes allow the herb's bioactive ingredients to be made available in an easily consumable form that's strong enough to have a physiological effect. Depending on the strength of the herbal preparation you made, your dosage will differ. This chapter discusses these details and more.

Extraction

Extraction was discussed in-depth in Chapter 5. Multiple forms of extraction were discussed. There are other forms of extraction that are used on an industrial scale that remove almost all bioactive ingredients from herbs for consumption. You will likely not perform these extraction techniques if you have a small or medium-sized business setup. Once you have a factory or industrial-level setup, this will likely change so that you can make your production processes more efficient.

Electric Field extraction is one of these industrial extraction processes. This is also called pulsed electric field extraction. It breaks down cell walls and is used as a pre-treatment to other extraction processes. This process significantly increases extraction yields of targeted compounds.

Ultrasound wave extraction makes use of these waves to obliterate plant walls. Very high quality extracts because it preserves all the molecules in the plant. Molecules that are preserved include vitamins, amino acids, enzymes, and proteins. In some cases, the plant is also ground through a mechanical mill before being strained to ensure maximum bioactive ingredient release.

There are other forms of industrial extraction, but the above methods result in high quality outputs. When creating a large enterprise based on herbal medicine, you will most likely consider using at least one of the above forms of extraction.

Expression

Expression is the process of pressing out the content of botanical material, such as a herb. It is done with a press of some sort—the press is often a specialized machine that has a combination between a squeezing mechanism, cutting mechanisms, and filtration devices. The result is high quality juice of the herb. This process has been used in many types of herbal health products, such as moringa concentrate created as a health supplement that complements nutrient deficient diets. Expression thus differs from extraction in that the bioactive content of a herb isn't transferred into another substance, but is rather squeezed out of the substance in question.

Fractionation

Fractionation is when the parts of a herbal extract or juice are separated into different parts. These parts are different components that are contained in the herbal extract. Some are heavier while some are lighter, allowing the mixture to be separated into parts. This is useful for testing because each fraction (or level) of the mix can then be purified for testing.

Purification

Purification is where each part or fraction of the extract is broken into its finer components. This makes it easier to determine what components make up the extract. Devices such as a centrifuge can be used to purify each component in the extract until all components have been separated and identified. Having identified the compounds in an extract, the herbalist or herbal firm will then be able to determine what benefits and side effects will spring from a particular herbal medicine.

Fermentation

Fermentation is good for getting herbs to last longer. It can give an enjoyable flavor to the herb when the herb is going to be used for food purposes. The flavor is tangy and fresh. Not only does fermentation give a unique flavor to the herb in question, it's also a good way of generating probiotics that can then be consumed to make the body healthier. This is a way of processing herbs so that you can benefit from them in a different way than you would in one of the above extraction techniques, or with drying, or with freezing.

It's easy to ferment herbs. All you need is the herb or herbs, brine (salt water), a jar for fermentation purposes, a fermentation lid (a lid designed to keep out as much air and oxygen as possible during the fermentation process, while releasing pressure buildup from bubbling), and fermentation weights (heavy objects used to keep the herbs submerged under the brine so that they don't get exposed to the air and rot).

You wash your herbs and remove the leaves from their stems. Pack the jar you'll be used for fermentation almost to the top with these leaves. Pour over the brine (normally made from filtered water and fine Celtic or Himalayan salt). Put in the weight so the leaves are kept under the brine's surface, then screw on your lid. There will be bubbling while you're fermenting the herbs, so put the jar on a surface where it will be okay for material to spill out. Then place the jar somewhere out of direct sunlight for five to 10 days. You'll know it's complete when there's no more bubbling.

Fermented herbs are then stored in jars for easy use. Use smaller jars for best results because a jar of fermented herbs will only last between a week and two weeks before it goes off. Thus, having multiple smaller jars will keep your fermented herb stock lasting longer. Jars that haven't been opened will remain viable for much longer than ones that have been opened.

Dosages of Herbs

Herbal dosage is something that varies according to the herb you take, the ailment or condition you take it for, and the strength of the medicinal preparation. There are, however, some general guidelines that can be followed. When using dried herbs, keep it to 5 grams per day at a maximum. This includes dried herbs that have been powdered. When you're using dried herbs for teas, use 5 grams as the guideline, unless your tea recipe directs otherwise. When using fresh herbs in a medicinal context, one can normally take up to

Herbal medicines that come in liquid form have a smaller daily dose. Tinctures are normally taken at 5 milliliters per day. Essential oils are very strong and should be kept to 5 drops per day. But, when taking essential oils, they need to be diluted in another oil or in water before taking them. Other forms of extract, such as glycosides and macerated oils should also be kept to about 5 milliliters per day. Your herbal practitioner or herbal practitioner guidelines might differ and will normally give you exact dosages for each type of herb, but this section provides general guidelines that will keep you safe until the point where you have an exact amount for each individual herb you use.

This chapter showed industrial extraction and quality control procedures used in herbalism. It also described how much of a herb to take. The next chapter will describe a few of the different ways Native Americans have incorporated herbs into their daily lives to remedy common issues.

CHAPTER 8

NATIVE AMERICAN HERBAL REMEDIES

There are a couple of popular remedies that have become integral into the Native American way of life. These remedies assist people with their daily medicinal and health needs, making their lives better. You can use them too to increase the quality of your life.

Tongue Wash

The latex or the leaf of jatropha gaumeri green (also known as pomolche) can assist with getting rid of oral candida. It's good for healing canker sores, treating tooth abscesses, soothing toothaches, and reducing swelling in your oral region. You can use this herb by making a hot infusion with the leaf of the plant that can then be used as a mouthwash. After rinsing out your mouth with the wash, use a tongue scraper to remove any residue still on your tongue. For good measure, you can take a second swig of mouthwash to rinse out anything left behind by the scraper.

Indigestion Tincture

That pain in your stomach after eating a heavy meal or something you can't digest easily can be quite uncomfortable. To remedy cases of indigestion, Native Americans have several tinctures that can help. Most of the herbs used for indigestion are classified as bitter herbs. Boldo, goldenseal, yarrow, and Oregon grape can all be used for indigestion (amongst other herbs). You simply make a tincture from one of these herbs or a blend of them by following the steps to make a tincture as described in Chapter 5.

Raspberry Tea

Raspberry tea is usually made using the leaves of the plant. You can also make tea from the fruit, but it's easier to use the leaves because they can be used fresh or dry. An easier way to use the fruit is in salads or by juicing them. Raspberry leaf tea can assist with multiple ailments and conditions, but it is particularly well known for helping with conditions and issues relating to the womb. It is used to make it more comfortable when giving birth, to make menstrual cramps less painful, and to increase the general health of the uterus. To make it, you simply follow the steps for making a hot infusion as described in Chapter 5.

Infusion of Sage

Much of the sage plant can be used for health reasons. It can be used in foods, such as in salad or as a spice. It is also used as a medicine, especially to regain vitality after giving birth. Burning sage is also said to have healing qualities. This practice is closely linked with spirituality, with the purpose of purifying the person, a home, a location, or a part of life. By following the steps in Chapter 5 about how to make an infusion (either hot or cold will work), you can ease irritation and inflammation in your throat, your chest, and your lungs. The infusion is a good remedy when you have a cold or an infection in your lungs.

Infusion of Dandelion Tea

Dandelion has been used by many Native American tribes for medicinal reasons. It's particularly good for calming down your body and mind, and for pain relief. Additional benefits when it's used as a tea are assisting digestive processes and aiding kidney health. Teas can be made by multiple parts of the plant, but the root is particularly effective when it comes to handling pain. You can chop up the root and roast it and then steep it in boiling water to get a coffee-like result. You can also chop it up and steep it in boiling water without roasting it for a strong herbal tea. You can also dry out chopped up roots and use it months after you harvested the plant—in which case you will also get a tea-like result.

Having seen that herbal remedies can easily be incorporated into your life in this chapter, you'll be able to learn how to forage them in the next chapter so that you have the herbs you need for life remedies.

CHAPTER 9

FORAGING NATIVE AMERICAN HERBALS

Foraging is the collection of plants from nature for their use in food and medicine. This is a practice that can be either just a passing interest, or an avid hobby, or a lifestyle. Humans have been foraging since before the days of cavepeople, and they continue to do so today, albeit at a lower percentage with the advent of food stores. Nevertheless, it remains an integral part to Native American herbalism because you can collect the herbs you need for medicine on foraging trips.

What is Foraging?

Foraging is an activity that's closely linked with nature. It incorporates outdoor expeditions to natural environments where collections of the herbs you desire to collect can be found. You go to the natural environment, take what you need in a sustainable way, then take it home with you to use in your medicines. The main advantages of foraging for your herbs rather than growing them or getting them from a store is that you're obtaining the herb in the environment they've adapted to live in. You're thus getting it as naturally pure as you possibly can.

Why Forage?

Foraging is good for you on a mental and physical level. You're getting out of the bustle of your life and getting into contact with nature. This automatically calms you down and allows you to disengage from the problems you face on a daily basis. By connecting with the world around you, your mind can revitalize itself, thereby allowing you to tackle your life's problems with renewed vigor once you've completed a foraging trip.

The physical benefits come from exercise and clean air. Foraging can be a physically demanding task. You're going over rough terrain a lot of the time, and you might end up walking for long distances. The air in these natural environments tends to be purer than city air. You don't have heavy sorcerers of air pollution around while foraging, so the air you breathe is cleaner. Not to mention the plants and in the wilderness purify the air pollution that is present, thus ensuring the air is clean.

Basic Laws of Foraging

Laws about foraging vary from state to state and nation to nation. You'll need to read up on the laws about foraging in your region to make sure you don't get on the wrong side of the law. There is normally a government department in charge of agriculture, forests, or environmental affairs that can be consulted if you have any questions. They often have websites that contain the most important laws that you'll need to follow. This section lists some guidelines that, when followed, will assist you in staying out of trouble with the law in most circumstances.

The first thing to do is to make sure you have gotten the approval of the person or people who have authority over the land you want to enter that you may forage there. This could be a park ranger if you intend on foraging at a national park. You might need to obtain a permit to do so. It would be the owner or renter if you want to forage on private property.

When getting their permission, you need to make sure you know what you're allowed to forage and the quantity limits that are placed on any type of foraged items. Ask the person you get permission from to confirm any queries you might have.

The second thing is to know what species are endangered and what species aren't endangered. Don't take species that are endangered because this is both unsustainable foraging, and it's most likely punishable by law. There could be species that you're not supposed to take at a particular park, even though that species isn't endangered on a national or international level. This is because the species could have a low quantity of specimens at that park. Know what species you aren't supposed to take when you're foraging at the park so that you don't get into any sort of trouble.

Ethics of Foraging

A reciprocal relationship with the land forms the basis of ethical foraging. Plant seeds when you see them and plant parts of trees or plants that have snapped off. Put mushrooms in mesh bags or baskets when you harvest them so their spores can travel throughout the nature area you've foraged in. Take steps to help propagate the plants that have sacrificed parts of themselves for you.

Ethical foraging also requires that you identify plants properly. Educate yourself about plants so that you can spot their characteristics. If you're not sure what plant you're looking at, don't harvest it. Further, only harvest what you need. Don't take what you don't need because others might need or want it. The plant needs to keep up its population, so taking more than a third of a plant patch or taking from the only patch of particular species in a nature zone can lead to destructive results.

Take steps to have a positive impact on the environment you're foraging in. Bring trash bags to pick up litter. Refill holes you create when digging up plants and don't make new tracks if you don't need to. Be conscientious towards the animals, nests, and natural spaces you find. Keep quiet as much as possible to keep noise pollution levels down.

Foraging Safety

Don't harvest close to pollution sources. Sources of pollution include large roads, airports, and factories (in terms of air pollution). Agricultural chemicals from commercial farms, such as pesticides, and industrial runoff are sources of water pollution. Refrain from harvesting around water sources close to commercial farms so that you don't unintentionally bring toxins and heavy metals into your health practices.

Safety also requires that you wear the correct type of clothing. This would include closed shoes, gloves, long pants, and socks. As a result, your body will be protected from toxins due to touch. Also take steps to be prepared for unfortunate eventualities. Steps would include having a field guide, some clean water, a snack, a power bank, pruners and some tools, and a map of the location you're foraging at.

Proper Identification

Notice what plants you're looking at and harvesting, because if you don't, you could accidentally take a poisonous one. There are characteristics you should observe about the herb and its parts. When it comes to the leaves, take note of their texture, color, shape, and growth pattern. Stalks should be examined as to stiffness, whether they're woody or non-woody, color, whether they're hollow or not, and whether there are spines or other things on the surface. Noting the branching pattern can also be of use.

Flowers can be distinguished using their color, size, shape, whether they cluster or not, and whether they're on a stiff stem or they're drooping. The fruit can be characterized by looking at its texture, shape, size, color, and whether it's a dry or juicy fruit. Some fruits also split open when they're ripe, which is also an identifying characteristic. The seeds can be told apart using color, design, size, shape, and whether they're winged or not.

You can use the roots as an identifying tool if you've removed the plant from the ground. Observe the depth of the roots, the color of their skin, the color inside the root, and whether it's a taproot or fibrous root. Finally, you can use the general aspect of a herb to determine what plant you're looking at. Look at the form, the width, and the height.

Sustainable Foraging

Sustainable foraging keeps the environment intact for future generations. Past generations didn't have the same concerns, to everyone's detriment. Learn about the environment, plants, and regulations on sustainability in your area. When trying a new herb, only take a small bit. Allergies or negative reactions can be ruled out using small quantities. This way you're not harvesting and reducing plant populations before you've even determined if you can take it. Plants need to have a large and stable enough grouping to grow and sustain themselves. Other foragers need some sort of grouping so that they can also take advantage of nature. Do what you can to make this a reality.

Keep an Eye on Your Surroundings

There are dangers in natural environments. This includes animals, poisonous plants and plant sap, and sharp rocks. You don't want to risk danger by not being aware of things such as this. Also look out for undisturbed areas that are havens for plants and critters. Don't enter these areas and safeguard them as much as you can so that you champion the health of truly wild spaces.

Essential Tools for Foraging

Bags are essential. Paper bags, mesh bags, and baskets are used for harvested mushrooms. Closed containers are used for leaves and twigs (but preferably not plastic bags as they will often wilt your herbs. You can also use cloth bags for harvested plant matter because it allows air to pass through so that the herbs overheat and wilt. A bucket is also a useful tool in this aspect. You can fill it part-way with water and close it off with a lid to transport your foraged materials without letting them go limp in the car.

Knives are useful. A digging knife can be used to take a plant out of the ground or to plant seeds and branches in the ground. A cutting knife, scissors, and pruners can all be used to snip off leaves, flowers, fruit, and seeds without damaging plants. Shovels are also good tools, particularly if they have a pointed end and are small enough to strap onto your belt.

You should also keep the safety equipment with you that's described in the "Foraging Safety" section earlier in this chapter. A compass or magnifying glass can be a useful addition for identifying plants and remaining safe.

Foraging as a High Level of Security

Food sovereignty is a vital intergroup issue at the moment. This is when cultural groups can eat according to their cultural food practices and can do so in a sustained way. This means there would be no need to rely on existing food structures, which takes demand off from existing food supply chains. It means that cultural groups don't need to eat the types of dishes provided in existing food supply chains.

Check Your Personal Tolerance

Take a small amount of a new herb every time. Make sure you've identified it correctly. Cooked herbs are less likely to produce negative reactions than fresh ones. Even non-toxic ones can give you reactions if you're allergic or intolerant to them.

The Do's and Don'ts of Foraging and Harvesting

This section contains some additional suggestions for making your foraging experience productive and sustainable. Follow them for better security for yourself and the environment.

Make Sure You Are Familiar With Plant Scientific Names

There are variations of almost each type of plant. These have different scientific names. Each has its own qualities—some are toxic while the rest are not. Different nutritional values and medicinal benefits are also observed from species to species of the same plant.

Avoid Using Plants That Are Unfamiliar to You

Test them first because you don't know if your body will tolerate every herb. If you have doubts about identifying the plant, ask someone who will be able to help. You don't want to consume the wrong type of plant. It might just be a toxic one and you don't know it.

Learn About the Environment That the Plant Grows In

This can be useful for identifying purposes. Things like climate, humidity, and elevation can help you find the plant you're looking for or to determine whether a particular type of plant will occur in the region at all.

Watch for Seasonal Variations

Seasonal variations differ in nutritional values from season to season. Some parts only occur in specific seasons (e.g. fruits and flowers). The plant might die down and be unavailable during certain seasons. It's useful to set up a foraging calendar with which herbs to forage in your environment, during which season.

Avoid Foraging in Hazardous Locations

You want to avoid injury in hazardous locations because it will be difficult for rescuers to get to you. You might have no cell signal, and if you have no map it's even worse. Cliffs, sticky mud, river rapids, and areas prone to predators are all hazardous locations.

Tidying Up the Plants

Broken branches lying around from cutting paths or trudging through flower clumps rather than going around them are messy. Remove the broken plant material and infected plants or leaves when you see them. By doing so, you can prevent the infection of the rest of the clump.

Never Take Plants That are Protected

First of all, this is illegal. Second of all, it's immoral. Plants need to have their own environment where they can be safe and they need your help improving their numbers. You should plant seeds or plant branches you see laying around. Rather than reducing them, you're increasing them by taking steps to plant them.

Do Not Remove the Plants

Take what you need from a location, but don't take the whole plant if you don't need the whole plant. If you need the whole plant, make sure there are other specimens and clumps of it around. Even when you take it, you might not need all the parts. If, for e.g., you don't need the roots, then leave them in the ground for the plant to regrow. The same applies to seed clusters.

List the Various Species

There will be multiple herb species in your area. Note where they occur and their prevalence in that location. This becomes a tool you can use later when you forage to find further herbs.

When to Gather Mushrooms

Mushrooms are a staple for foods that we forage. They're a good source of nutrition and sometimes a great source of medicinal benefits. It's commonly best to find them around October and surrounding months in the Northern Hemisphere. The best time of day is in the middle of the night or colder parts of the day. There are variations between mushrooms, so consulting your field guide is best when harvesting.

This chapter showed how to forage and how to stay safe while doing so. The next chapter will take a closer look at the topic, specifically wildcrafting.

CHAPTER 10

WILDCRAFTING NATIVE AMERICAN HERBAL

Wildcrafting is a skill you can cultivate. Native Americans have perfected this skill for thousands of years. Following the suggestions from this chapter and the previous chapter, you can be an effective wildcrafter that knows how to get the plants you need.

What Is Wildcrafting?

Wildcrafting is very similar to foraging. The focus, however, is more precise with wildcrafting than with foraging. Foraging includes gathering plants, fish, and animal products from the wild. The main purpose of foraging is related to consumption of food. What's more, many would include gathering plants and other things from natural spaces in urban areas as foraging activities (e.g. gathering herbs from your local botanical gardens).

Wildcrafting, however, is more focused on gathering plants than animal products, and it's more focused on gathering plants for medicinal purposes than food purposes. There are many perks to wildcrafting, the main one being that you become self-sufficient when it comes to your everyday medical care. Further benefits are that you know where the herbs came from that you're using in your medicine, and you know that you chose high quality, fresh specimens. In other words, you know you're not getting the dross of medicine production firms.

Some people use the term wildcrafting interchangeably with foraging, while others classify them as completely separate practices. In this book we take the approach that wildcrafting is simply the focused collection of plants for medicinal use from wild spaces, whereas foraging is collecting plants and animal products from any natural area for food or medicinal purposes.

Core Principle of Wildcrafting

Being at one with nature is the basis of wildcrafting. A spiritual or emotional connection is cultivated. Herbs are seen as more than just plants, but rather as living beings. Wildcrafting aims to improve your senses so that you're better connected with the environment. Being in tune with the world around you rather than just the plants you're harvesting is one of the main purposes of wildcrafting.

The Basics of Wildcrafting

There are additional basics for wildcrafting that you should know. These basics are additions to the rules and basics you learned about in the foraging chapter.

Know How to Cut

If you don't cut right, you'll damage the plant. Damage could make it difficult for the plant to continue growing. Cutting properly could encourage growth, such as when cutting a distance away from a node. Some plants grow better when cut at an angle, while others grow better when cutting straight across. Just breaking off a branch is probably the most harmful with thick-branched plants. Know how to cut plants so that you contribute to their drive for survival.

Opportunism

In wildcrafting, this word is not used in a negative sense. Taking some of it for your garden, then planting it at home or a nearby nature zone are ways to make the plant more accessible to you. If you've planted it in your garden, you'll have less reason to go out and take it from the wild. Thus you're self-sufficiently growing your own source of the herb. This is especially a good idea when land is going to be developed and plants are going to be destroyed in that nature zone. The term to use is 'stewardship.'

Offer Gratitude to the Sacred Plants

Wildcrafting is about a spiritual connection. Connecting with something larger than yourself and respecting mother nature is integral to this practice. Native Americans hold deep reverence for the natural world, so wildcrafters try to emulate this. Asking permission and saying thank you to the plant when you're harvesting from it is something that you can do to build on that spiritual connection. Many will also make an offering, such as planting seeds, or watering the plant, or taking away litter around the herb stand.

Wildcrafting Tips

Wildcrafting can be a family activity or a fun activity with friends. You spend time together doing interesting things that differ from your daily activities. There are no cell phones or other distractions present. Those participating are forced to share close communication.

Be aware of the seasons. General season guidelines follow. Spring is great for leaves and stems, and late spring is good for flowers and buds. Summer is good for flowers and fruit. Fall is good for fruit, seeds, and fungi, while late autumn is ideal for roots and underground plant structures like rhizomes. Winter is good for winter-growing plants.

Walk slowly so that you observe your environment. Notice things you normally wouldn't. Examine surroundings you are familiar with from a different perspective, almost taking on a scholarly perspective.

Know that you might not find a particular plant that you set out to find. There will probably be other plants not on your list that you could harvest. Be versatile with what you could collect. Observe an adventure, then you'll find multiple things you could potentially use—rather than being boxed in.

Weeds and common plants can be a good source of medicine, so don't ignore them. Some of the best medicines come from weeds, e.g. dandelion root tea. Weeds are also more common and don't have to be safeguarded from underpopulation. It's okay to remove invasive species altogether, so you can harvest those without abandon.

Reasons to Start Wildcrafting

Wildcrafting often leads to weeds being harvested for their useful qualities. This is good for the environment because there are less invasive species using resources of native species. These weeds, and other herbs you wildcraft, are very good for you. You will find that some are even considered to be superfoods. Why not make use of this source of organic, non-GMO medicine.

It's cost-effective to wildcraft. You're not spending hundreds or thousands of dollars on medication. Rather, you're spending the money you need for fuel or transport and for any wildcrafting equipment you need. Plus, once you have all the equipment you need (which isn't necessarily all the prescribed equipment), you won't have any further equipment expenses.

If you take kids with you, you'll be providing them with

hours of educational fun. Not only this, but they'll understand and respect nature more. In the process of doing this, you're passing along knowledge that they can use for the rest of their lives.

This chapter gave you an overview of how and why you would do wildcrafting. In the next chapter we'll look at some of the conditions you can treat using the herbs you gathered while wildcrafting.

CHAPTER 11

DISEASES YOU CAN TREAT USING NATIVE AMERICAN MEDICINE

Native American herbal culture has been honed into a precise and useful alternative medicine over a period of many years. In chapter two we looked at some of the conditions you can improve using Native American herbalism. In this chapter we're going to look at conditions that aren't only alleviated with Native American herbalism, but that can be cured in most cases.

Insomnia

Insomnia is the inability to sleep or the quality of struggling to fall asleep. It usually refers to when this occurs over protracted periods of time, or if it's habitual. There are multiple herbs that are known to be good for insomnia, such as ashwagandha and lavender.

Anxiety

Anxiety is a condition in which you feel nervous about many things, specifically when excessively so. It leads you to avoid doing things you know you needed to or than you know would have been good for you to do. You might feel that there are threats lurking around when there aren't actually any. Anxiety could be centered around specific people, places, situations, or subjects (such as an overwhelming fear of socializing with strangers), or it could be generalized (as in the

221

case of generalized anxiety disorder). There are also physical phenomena you might experience, such as rigid muscles, that indicate you're in flight mode.

Conventional medications for this have many side effects. They also commonly have an excessive price—a price that's unaffordable for lower middle class or financially challenged individuals. Herbal medication can be made for anxiety that has a far lower cost and that's much more gentle on the body. You just need the right herbs and recipes about how to prepare those herbs. Examples of herbs that are often used to overcome anxiety are chamomile and lavender.

Fever

Fever is when your body has a very high temperature, specifically around the head or forehead regions. It's accompanied by other physical phenomena, such as shaking, shivering, or sweating excessively. Mental states might also result from severe instances, such as confusion or seeing things that aren't there. Fevers occur in relation with many health conditions, with one of the more common ones being influenza (i.e. flu).

Herbs have been used by Native Americans to break fevers. Some induce sweating, which helps to cool down the body. Others attack the fever using a different chemical approach or process. Some of the herbs that are used most commonly as fever solutions are yarrow, echinacea, and elderflower.

Irregularities of the Menstrual Cycle and Cramps

Menstrual irregularities can be painful, embarrassing, and messy. It can affect other parts of your life. Native Americans had many solutions for this. Multiple herbs can be used for this condition. What's more, they're not harsh on the system and they don't negatively affect your hormones. Commonly used herbs for this purpose are ginger and raspberry leaf.

Abscess and Gingivitis

Abscesses are swollen, pussy sacks in the body. They're a sign of infection and can occur in multiple parts of the body. They commonly occur on the gums. Gingivitis is inflammation of the gums. It's commonly caused by infections, just as abscesses are caused by infection. Both conditions can effectively be handled with herbal means. Some herbs for these conditions are slippery elm, lapacho, and burdock.

Back Pain

Back pain is common in the working world. Exercise is one of the best solutions, but herbal medicine is a great addition to proper exercise. It helps with inflammation and pain, as well as with the process of building up muscles and strengthening bones. Examples of herbs that are often used for back pain are ginger, liquorice, and Solomon's seal root. You can use them either in ointments, compresses, or paultices for topical application, or in teas, capsules, and tinctures for internal consumption.

Diarrhea

Diarrhea is a common condition, especially in our current world of fast food (including fast food made in conditions that aren't necessarily always hygienic). It consists of runny feces and difficulty controlling yourself from defecating. You might want to pass gas, and then end up with feces coming out. This isn't a new problem. Native Americans use multiple herbs and plants to help bind the feces so that your defecation occurs in a way it's supposed to.

The herbs used for diarrhea are often of the kind that form a mucilage when they come into contact with liquid. This binds the juices that would consist of runny diarrhea so that it comes out as a firm mass. Herbs and plants often used to accomplish this are blackberry, raspberry, and psyllium husk.

Constipation

This is the opposite to diarrhea. It consists of difficulty passing feces, normally because feces are dry. You can sit on the toilet for a long time with nothing happening, even though you feel the urge to defecate. Native Americans have many solutions for this. Commonly used herbs for constipation are peppermint, dandelion, and liquorice.

Cough

Coughing passes air and other things from the lungs in a forceful way. This body function is present in a variety of illnesses and diseases. Irritants enter the lungs, such as microorganisms, resulting in infections, colds and flus. Herbs can be used to soothe the throat including marshmallow, slippery elm, and echinacea. Herbs can also be used to ease tight chest muscles, such as using anise hyssop. Herbs can also be used to help with inflammation in the lungs, throat, and esophagus, for example stinging nettle.

Depression

Depression is a crippling condition in which you feel apathetic and like there's no hope. You might feel guilty and that you're not good enough. The things you do seem pointless, but you do them anyway. You might get to the point where you do nothing at all because you don't see the point in it all. There are multiple forms of depression, some being around specific life situations, some having to do with the time frame you've been depressed, and yet others having to do with the intensity of the condition. St. John's Wort is one example out of many herbs that can help overcome depression.

Acne

Acne is a skin condition that normally affects teenagers and young adults, although some older individuals also experience it. The glands in your face that produce the oily substance called "sebum" get infected or inflamed. The result is that your face (and many times other parts of the body) becomes covered in red and white pimple heads that often pop and become a pockmark-like scar tissue later in life. A plant that's commonly used for acne (even in commercial products) is witch hazel.

This chapter covered various conditions that can be cured with herbs. The next chapter will give you some safety tips for using Native American herbs.

CHAPTER 12

SAFETY TIPS FOR USING NATIVE AMERICAN HERBS

Safety is of concern in herbal medicine. You're not always part of the supply chains that provide your herbal supplements, therefore you're not able to enforce your quality standards as closely as you would otherwise. There is scanty legislation on herbal medicine, resulting in unscrupulous individuals doing unethical things (such as providing toxic supplements) with little to no punishment. This is a short chapter with suggestions for you to follow so that you safely care for your health with herbs.

Tips for Using Herbal Products Safely

Buy or use herbal products from a qualified practitioner or reputable supplier. They've proven their mettle to many individuals, plus they need to keep remaining reliable if they want to maintain their reputation. Ask for products that are clearly labeled, wherever you get them from. Things you should expect to see on labels are safety information, directions for use, dosage, quantity, the date of manufacture, the name of the product, and a batch number.

Avoid using over-the-counter products from a health food shop, pharmacy or the internet. You don't know who or what provided them.

Talk to your doctor and complementary health practitioner when you intend to start on a new herb. This is particularly important if you take other types of herbs or medication, when pregnant, or when breastfeeding. If you're taking a new herb and you experience undesirable reactions, contact your medical practitioner to ask for their direction to prevent unwanted circumstances from developing.

When you're undergoing medical treatment or you're on medication, be on the lookout for any undesirable reactions. Herbs may be natural, but not all of them are safe. Some are toxic, and with some a part of the herb is toxic. Even non-toxic herbs can produce unwanted effects in people with allergies or when mixing with other medication you're taking.

Examples of herbs that cause interactions include St. John's wort, black cohosh, ginkgo biloba, garlic, and green tea. St. John's wort is used mainly for depression (for which purpose it can be highly effective), but it can stop chemotherapy and other drugs from working properly. Black cohosh can cause liver problems for people who have a history of liver problems or liver damage. Both ginkgo biloba and garlic can cause risk for those who are going to undergo surgery in the next two weeks, especially if they have a history of a low platelet count. Green tea can interact with Bortezomib, a cancer drug used to treat multiple myeloma and mantle cell lymphoma, and prevent it from working.

There are other interactions and dangers possible when taking herbs. The solution to prevent this is to know what herb you're taking, what it's for, and how much of it to take. Heed safety instructions of your medical practitioner. By following the straightforward tips above, you can ensure you safely benefit from herbs.

CONCLUSION

Herbalism is making use of herbs from nature for the purpose of healing. You use natural substances that are less harsh than conventional medicines. These natural substances are also cheaper and easier to access than many medicinal drugs. Not only this, but they conform with cultural practices and traditions that stretch back for thousands of years.

Herbalism and foraging both engender a respect for nature. The environment is brought into your home, and in the process you're learning to appreciate the natural world rather than the artificial physical world. In this book you learned that by foraging and wildcrafting you can take control of your food and medical health requirements. In the process, you're independently looking after your physical and mental health. The result is that you develop a lifestyle of being in control of your own health.

Many everyday remedies were discussed in this book. There were also some remedies for situations you wouldn't face on a daily basis, but that you nevertheless could use a medical remedy for. These remedies are all accessible, easy to make, and can be obtained through multiple sources. You can grow your own herbs, buy them from a supplier, or you can forage for them in wild spaces.

With the tools in this book, you've laid the groundwork for

a future as a successful herbalist. You can improve your health and the health of those around you. Use these tools to take medical care to the next level in your life!

REFERENCES

NATIVE AMERICAN HISTORY: ACCURATE & COMPREHENSIVE HISTORY, ORIGINS, CULTURE, TRIBES, LEGENDS, MYTHOLOGY, WARS, STORIES & MORE OF THE NATIVE INDIGENOUS AMERICANS

AHA STAFF. (2009, November 16). Inuit contact: An arctic culture teaching resource. Perspectives on History. www.historians.org/publications-and-directories/perspectives-on-history/november-2009/inuit-contact-an-arctic-culture-teaching-resource

Asikinack, W. (n.d). Sun Dance: Indigenous saskatchewan encyclopedia - university of saskatchewan. Teaching.usask.ca. www.teaching.usask.ca/indigenoussk/import/sun_dance.php

Awali. (2016, November 1). Democracy and the iroquois constitution. Field Museum. www.fieldmuseum.org/blog/democracy-and-iroquois-constitution

Bleiweis, S. (2013). The downfall of the iroquois. Emory Endeavors in History 2013. http://history.emory.edu/home/documents/endeavors/volume5/gunpowder-age-v-bleiweis.pdf

Browner, T. (2019). Powwow: Native american celebration. Encyclopædia Britannica. www.britannica.com/topic/powwow

Canadian Museum of History. (n.d.). Traditional Stories and Creation Stories | Canadian History Hall. https://www.historymuseum.ca/history-hall/traditional-and-creation-stories/#:~:text=First%20Peoples%20remember%20their%20origins

Carlisle, J. D. (2020, October 20). TSHA: Choctaw indians. www.tshaonline.org/handbook/entries/choctaw-indians

Carlysue. (2017, November 8). Did the indigenous americans take a ride on the kelp highway? National Geographic Education Blog. blog.education.nationalgeographic.org/2017/11/08/did-the-first-americans-take-a-ride-on-the-kelp-highway/

Chesnutt, B. (2021). Bering land bridge: Evidence & migration. Study.com. study.com/academy/lesson/bering-land-bridge-evidence-migration.html

Chiblaw, S. (2021, December). Research framework based on the anishinaabe. Research Gate. www.researchgate.net/figure/Research-framework-based-on-the-Anishinaabe-Cree-Medicine-Wheel-Holistic-health_fig1_341257600

Choctaw nation. (n.d.). Heritage & Traditions. ChoctawNation.

www.choctawnation.com/history-culture/heritage-traditions

Choctaw tribe. (2012, November 20). WarPaths2PeacePipes. www.warpaths2peacepipes.com/indian-tribes/choctaw-tribe.htm

Christian, D. (n.d.). Recordkeeping and history. KhanAcademy. www.khanacademy.org/humanities/big-history-project/agriculture-civilization/first-cities-appear/a/recordkeeping-and-history

Clothing. (n.d.) Cree Natives. cree-natives.weebly.com/clothing.html

Colonialism. (n.d.) Indigenouspeoplesatlasofcanada. indigenouspeoplesatlasofcanada.ca/article/colonialism/

Coyle, M. (n.d.). Marginalized by sui generis - duress, undue influence and crown-aboriginal treaties. Manitoba Law Journal, vol. 32, no. 2, 2022, p. 34, www.canlii.org/en/commentary/doc/2008CanLIIDocs192#

Cree. (2019, April 6). In Wikipedia. en.wikipedia.org/wiki/Cree

Cross, A. (1990). Raven and the indigenous men from conception to completion.

Cultural traditions of native American hunting and gathering. (2020, April). TribalTrade. tribaltradeco.com/blogs/teachings/cultural-traditions-of-native-american-hunting-and-gathering

Cultures & traditions: Zapotec (Monte Albán). (n.d.). CollectionsDMA. collections.dma.org/essay/BnlpA3QY

Definition of HOMININ. (n.d.). www.merriam-Webster.com, www.merriam-webster.com/dictionary/hominin

Early human migrations. (2019, May 16). In Wikipedia. https://en.wikipedia.org/wiki/Early_human_migrations

Erlandson, J. M. (2007, October 30). The kelp highway hypothesis: marine ecology, the coastal migration theory, and the peopling of the americas. The Journal of Island and Coastal Archaeology, vol. 2, no. 2. pp. 161–174, 10.1080/15564890701628612

European contact. (n.d.) Haida History. sites.google.com/site/haidahistory/european-contact

Evans, A. C. (2022). Zapotec rituals, symbols & animal calendar. Study. study.com/academy/lesson/zapotec-rituals-symbols-animal-calendar.html

Fen M. (2019, December 18). The story of how humans came to the americas is constantly evolving. SmithsonianMag. www.smithsonianmag.com/science-nature/how-humans-came-to-americas-180973739/

Freeman, Milton. (2018). Arctic indigenous peoples in Canada. TheCanadianEncyclopedia. www.thecanadianencyclopedia.ca/en/article/aboriginal-people-arctic

French and iroquois wars (1642-1698). (2019) Uswars. www.uswars.net/french-iroquois-wars/

Gadacz, René R. (2019). Potlatch. TheCanadianEncyclopedia. www.thecanadianencyclopedia.ca/en/article/potlatch

Gadacz, René R. (2012, March 7). Snowshoes. TheCanadianEncyclopedia. www.thecanadianencyclopedia.ca/en/article/snowshoes

Gadacz, René R. (2021, April 2). Tipi. TheCanadianEncyclopedia. www.thecanadianencyclopedia.ca/en/article/tipi

Gardiner, L. (2010). Inuit culture, traditions, and history. Windows2Universe. www.windows2universe.org/earth/polar/inuit_culture.html

Gibbons, A. (2010). The human family's earliest ancestors. SmithsonianMag. www.smithsonianmag.com/science-nature/the-human-familys-earliest-ancestors-7372974/

Gitchi manitou. (n.d.). NativeLanguages. www.native-languages.org/gitchi-manitou.htm

Haida. (n.d.) NewWorldEncyclopedia. www.newworldencyclopedia.org/entry/Haida

Haida the land and the people. (2019). Civilization. www.historymuseum.ca/cmc/exhibitions/aborig/haida/hapso01e.html

Haida tribe. (2017). Warpaths2Peacepipes. www.warpaths2peacepipes.com/indian-tribes/haida-tribe.htm

Hall, A. J. (2017). Treaties with Indigenous peoples in Canada. The Canadian Encyclopedia. www.thecanadianencyclopedia.ca/en/article/aboriginal-treaties

Haudenosaunee guide for educators. (n.d.). Smithsonian Institution National Museum of the American Indian. https://americanindian.si.edu/sites/1/files/pdf/education/HaudenosauneeGuide.pdf

Hiawatha legendary onondaga chief. (n.d.). Britannica. www.britannica.com/topic/Hiawatha

Hileary, C. (2017, June 19). Native americans call for rethink of bering strait theory. VOA. www.voanews.com/a/native-americans-call-for-rethink-of-bering-strait-theory/3901792.html

Historic centre of oaxaca and archaeological site of monte albán. (n.d.). UNESCO World Heritage Centre. Unesco. whc.unesco.org/en/list/415/

Huang, A. (2011). Totem poles. IndigenousFoundations.ArtsUBC. indigenousfoundations.arts.ubc.ca/totem_poles/

Impact of non-indigenous activities on the inuit. (n.d.). Heritage.nf. www.heritage.nf.ca/articles/indigenous/inuit-impacts.php

Indian Mounds of Mississippi: National Register of Historic Places Travel Itinerary. (n.d.). Building the mounds. National Park Service. www.nps.gov/nr/travel/mounds/mounds.htm

Indigenous peoples of the pacific northwest coast. (2019, October 8). In Wikipedia. https://en.wikipedia.org/wiki/Indigenous_peoples_of_the_Pacific_Northwest_Coast

Johnston, B. (n.d.). The creation story of kitche manitou (the great spirit) of the ojibwe

Kennedy, D., Bouchard, R., & Gessler, T. (2010, October 24). Haida. The Canadian Encyclopedia. https://www.thecanadianencyclopedia.ca/en/article/haida-native-group

Kilroy-Ewbank, L. (n.d.). Mesoamerica, an introduction. KhanAcademy. www.khanacademy.org/humanities/art-americas/beginners-guide-art-of-the-americas/mesoamerica-beginner/a/mesoamerica-an-introduction

Kitz, T. (2019, September 26). Timeline of canadian colonialism and indigenous resistance. The Leveller. leveller.ca/2019/09/timeline-of-canadian-colonialism-and-indigenous-resistance/

Koehler, S. (2017, September 26). How environmental racism affects indigenous communities in the USA. WearYourVoiceMag. www.wearyourvoicemag.com/environmental-racism-affects-indigenous-communities-usa/

Laban Hinton, A. (2014). Colonial genocide in indigenous north america. Duke University Press. www.dukeupress.edu/colonial-genocide-in-indigenous-north-america

Little, B. (2020, March 5). How did humans evolve. History. www.history.com/news/humans-evolution-neanderthals-denisovans

Mary, L. (2012). Cree. FourDirectionsTeachings. www.fourdirectionsteachings.com/transcripts/cree.html

Merriam-Webster. (2014). Definition of genocide. Merriam-Webster. www.merriam-webster.com/dictionary/genocide

Merriam-Webster. (2019). Definition of sovereignty. Merriam-Webster. www.merriam-webster.com/dictionary/sovereignty

Merriam-Webster. (n.d.). Definition of time immemorial. Merriam-Webster. www.merriam-webster.com/dictionary/since%20time%20immemorial

Mitla: The zapotec place of the dead. (2020, December 12). HeritageDaily. www.heritagedaily.com/2020/12/mitla-the-zapotec-place-of-the-dead/136448

Mohawk. (2019). Britannica. www.britannica.com/topic/Mohawk

Morgan, O.L. (2016, August 2). Haudenosaunee (Iroquois) Peacemaking Protocol.

Morlan, R. E. (2006, February 6). Beringia. CanadianEncyclopedia. www.thecanadianencyclopedia.ca/en/article/beringia

Native american lands: Ownership and governance. (n.d.). Revenuedata. revenuedata.doi.gov/how-revenue-works/native-american-ownership-governance/

Native americans describe traditional views of land ownership. (n.d.). Social History for Every Classroom. Shec.ashp.cuny. shec.ashp.cuny.edu/items/show/1543

Native knowledge 360° frequently asked questions. (n.d.). National Museum of the American Indian. americanindian.si.edu/nk360/faq/did-you-know

Northwest coast native settings. (n.d.). HistoryMuseum. www.historymuseum.ca/cmc/exhibitions/aborig/nwca/nwcam10e.html

OECD. (n.d.). Overview of indigenous governance in canada: Evolving relations and key issues and debates linking indigenous communities with regional development in canada. OECD-ILibrary. www.oecd-ilibrary.org/sites/b4446f31-en/index.html?itemId=/content/component/b4446f31-en

Parks Canada Agency, G. of C. (2018, February 13). An Anishinaabe creation story - Pukaskwa National Park. Www.pc.gc.ca. https://www.pc.gc.ca/en/pn-np/on/pukaskwa/culture/autochtone-indigenous/recit-story

Powell, W. (2012). Native american creation stories. Americanyawp. www.americanyawp.com/reader/the-new-world/indian-creation-stories/

Preston, R. J. (2018, May 18). Nehiyawak Cree. The Canadian Encyclopedia. www.thecanadianencyclopedia.ca/en/article/cree

Raven Reads. (2018, November 29). The Raven in Haida Culture. Raven Reads Books Ltd. https://ravenreads.org/blogs/news/the-raven-in-haida-culture

Reich, D. (2018). Clovis people spread to central and south america, then vanished. HHMI. www.hhmi.org/news/clovis-people-spread-central-and-south-america-then-vanished

Robinson, A. (2018, April 5). Trickster. The Canadian Encyclopedia. www.thecanadianencyclopedia.ca/en/article/trickster

Robinson, A. (2018, March 20). Vision quest. The Canadian Encyclopedia. www.thecanadianencyclopedia.ca/en/article/vision-quest

S. Jesse. (2018). History and future of the book the power of indigenous storytelling. USask. words.usask.ca/historyofthebook2018/2018/09/22/the-power-of-indigenous-storytelling/

Saplakoglu, Y. (2019, August 29). Oldest evidence of north american settlement may have been found in idaho. Live Science. www.livescience.com/america-settlement-was-by-boat.html

Stinson, J. (n.d.). What are indigenous and western ways of knowing?

Residential schools. (2019, January 14). The Canadian Encyclopedia. www.thecanadianencyclopedia.ca/en/timeline/residential-schools

The dene nation. (n.d.). Land of the people. Dene Nation. denenation.com

The Editors of Encyclopedia Britannica. (2019, January 14). Iroquois confederacy definition, significance, history, & facts. Britannica. www.britannica.com/topic/Iroquois-Confederacy

The sun dance sacred ceremony. (2019, December 2).

NotesFromTheFrontier. www.notesfromthefrontier.com/post/the-sun-dance-sacred-ceremony

The zapotec world civilization. (n.d.). LumenLearning. courses.lumenlearning.com/suny-hccc-worldcivilization/chapter/the-zapotec/

Tjepkema, M. (2019, December 18). Life expectancy of first nations, métis and inuit household populations in canada. Government of Canada, Statistics Canada. StatCan.GC. www150.statcan.gc.ca/n1/pub/82-003-x/2019012/article/00001-eng.htm

Traditional clothing. (n.d.). IndigenousPeoplesAtlasofCanada. indigenouspeoplesatlasofcanada.ca/article/clothing/

Traditional medicine: Tobacco. (2021, January 21). CreeHealth. creehealth.org/health-tips/traditional-medicine-tobacco

Tuttle, R. H. (2019, January 8). Human evolution stages & timeline. Britannica. www.britannica.com/science/human-evolution

United Nations Declaration on the Rights of Indigenous Peoples (n.d.). United Nations for Indigenous Peoples. UN. https://www.un.org/development/desa/indigenouspeoples/declaration-on-the-rights-of-indigenous-peoples.html

United Nations Department of Economic and Social Affairs Indigenous Peoples. (2016, October 14). Free Prior and Informed Consent – An Indigenous Peoples' right and a good practice for local communities — FAO. United Nations. https://www.un.org/development/desa/indigenouspeoples/publications/2016/10/free-prior-and-informed-consent-an-indigenous-peoples-right-and-a-good-practice-for-local-communities-fao/#:~:text=FPIC%20is%20a%20principle%20protected

Walker, G. (2016, September 6). Aztec creation story. IndigenousPeople. www.indigenouspeople.net/aztecs.htm

Zasibley. (2015, February 17). Potlatch ceremonies and the repatriation of potlatch regalia theirs or ours. Vassar. pages.vassar.edu/theirsorours/2015/02/17/potlatch-ceremonies-and-the-repatriation-of-potlatch-regalia/

NATIVE AMERICAN HERBALISM: IMPROVE YOUR HEALTH, WELLNESS & VITALITY WITH INDIGENOUS HEALING PRACTICES, MEDICINAL PLANTS, NATURAL HERBS, & HERBALIST REMEDIES

Abdel-Aziz, S. M., Aeron, A., & Kahil, T. A. (2016). *Health benefits and possible risks of herbal medicine. Microbes in Food and Health*, 97–116. https://doi.org/10.1007/978-3-319-25277-3_6

Abubakar, A., & Haque, M. (2020). *Preparation of medicinal plants: Basic extraction and fractionation procedures for experimental purposes. Journal of Pharmacy and Bioallied Sciences*, 12(1), 1.

https://doi.org/10.4103/jpbs.jpbs_175_19

How to properly clean your tongue. (n.d.). Dr. Emma Wu and Associates Dentistry and Aesthetics. https://dremmawu.com/how-to-properly-clean-your-tongue/

Alfaro, D. (2020, January 10). *What are herbs, and how are they different from spices?* The Spruce Eats. https://www.thespruceeats.com/what-are-herbs-995714

Alieta. (2014, October 6). *How to make glycerine extracts.* Mountain Rose Herbs. https://blog.mountainroseherbs.com/make-glycerin-extracts-glycerites

Altramarca, G. & D. A. (n.d.). *Ultrasonic extraction.* Albrigi in Hebra. https://albrigiinherba.com/contacts/extraction/ultrasonic-extraction/

Arizona Poison and Drug Information Center. (n.d.). P*oisonous plants of the Verde Valley.* United States Department of Agriculture. chrome-extension://efaidnbmnnnibpcajpcglclefindmkaj/https://www.fs.usda.gov/Internet/FSE_DOCUMENTS/stelprdb5349883.pdf

Badger, A. (2018, October 3). *Root medicine: An herbalist's guide to digging roots.* Urban Moonshine. https://www.urbanmoonshine.com/blogs/blog/root-medicine-herbalist-guide-dig-roots

Balekundri, A., & Mannur, V. (2020). *Quality control of the traditional herbs and herbal products: a review.* Future Journal of Pharmaceutical Sciences, 6(1). https://doi.org/10.1186/s43094-020-00091-5

Banerjee, P. S. (2019, July 23). *Home remedies for chest congestion.* Med India. https://www.medindia.net/homeremedies/chest-congestion.asp

Bauer, B. A. (2018, March 2). *Herbal treatment for anxiety: Is it effective?* Mayo Clinic. https://www.mayoclinic.org/diseases-conditions/generalized-anxiety-disorder/expert-answers/herbal-treatment-for-anxiety/faq-20057945

Belwal, T., Ezzat, S. M., Rastrelli, L., Bhatt, I. D., Daglia, M., Baldi, A., Devkota, H. P., Orhan, I. E., Patra, J. K., Das, G., Anandharamakrishnan, C., Gomez-Gomez, L., Nabavi, S. F., Nabavi, S. M., & Atanasov, A. G. (2018). *A critical analysis of extraction techniques used for botanicals: Trends, priorities, industrial uses and optimization strategies.* TrAC Trends in Analytical Chemistry, 100, 82–102. https://doi.org/10.1016/j.trac.2017.12.018

Bog labrador tea: Overview, uses, side effects, & more. (n.d.). Web MD. https://www.webmd.com/vitamins/ai/ingredientmono-539/bog-labrador-tea

Bose, S. (2021, June 17). *Herbs for acne: Benefits and how to use them?* Be Beautiful India. https://www.bebeautiful.in/all-things-skin/skin-concerns/herbs-for-acne

Bradley, K. (2015, March 17). *Drying medicinal herbs.* Wonderground. https://wonderground.press/howto/drying-medicinal-herbs/

Brennan, D. (Ed.). (2021, June 23). *What Is an herbalist?* WebMD. https://www.webmd.com/a-to-z-guides/what-is-an-herbalist

Brinckmann, J., & Engels, G. (n.d.). *Chamomile. Herbalgram*, 108, 8–17. American Botanical Council. https://www.herbalgram.org/resources/herbalgram/issues/108/table-of-contents/hg108-herbpro-chamomile/

Brown, K. (2017, May 8). *Wildcrafting with kids: What you need to know.* Learning Herbs. https://learningherbs.com/skills/wildcrafting-with-kids/

Bryant, C. W. (n.d.). *What is the universal edibility test?* How Stuff Works. https://adventure.howstuffworks.com/universal-edibility-test.htm

Carpentieri, S., Režek Jambrak, A., Ferrari, G., & Pataro, G. (2022). *Pulsed electric field-assisted extraction of aroma and bioactive compounds from aromatic plants and food by-products.* Frontiers in Nutrition, 8. https://doi.org/10.3389/fnut.2021.792203

Cashman, K., & Beth, M. (2004, November 23). *Yew.* Bellarmine. https://www.bellarmine.edu/faculty/drobinson/yew.htm

CBR. (2020, December 10). *Nicotiana clevelandii.* Lady Bird Johnson Wildflower Center; The University of Texas at Austin. https://www.wildflower.org/plants/result.php?id_plant=NICL

Chadwick, M., Trewin, H., Gawthrop, F., & Wagstaff, C. (2013). *Sesquiterpenoids Lactones: Benefits to Plants and People.* International Journal of Molecular Sciences, 14(6), 12780–12805. https://doi.org/10.3390/ijms140612780

Cholesterol. (n.d.). Medline Plus. https://medlineplus.gov/cholesterol.html

Cleveland's tobacco. (n.d.). PictureThis. https://www.picturethisai.com/wiki/Nicotiana_clevelandii.html

Cleveland's tobacco: Nicotiana clevelandii. (n.d.). California Native Plant Society; Calscape. https://calscape.org/Nicotiana-clevelandii-()

Codekas, C. (2015, August 4). *How to make an herb and flower drying screen.* Herbal Academy. https://theherbalacademy.com/how-to-make-an-herb-and-flower-drying-screen/

Codekas, C. (2016, August 5). *6 tips for storing dried herbs.* Herbal Academy. https://theherbalacademy.com/6-tips-for-storing-dried-herbs/

Coffeeberry - Frangula californica. (n.d.). Calscape; California Native Plant Society. https://calscape.org/Frangula-californica-()

Complementary therapies - Therapies using herbs and plants. (n.d.). Cancer Council Victoria. https://www.cancervic.org.au/living-with-cancer/common-side-effects/complementary-therapies/herbs-plants.html

Complimentary and alternative medicine: Slippery elm. (n.d.). St. Luke's

Hospital. https://www.stlukes-stl.com/health-content/medicine/33/000274.htm

Corey-Pine, S. (2017, August 10). *Maceration vs. percolation: An important distinction.* Pine's Herbals. https://pinesherbals.com/new-blog/2017/8/10/maceration-vs-percolation-an-important-distinction

Cruz Martínez, C., Diaz Gómez, M., & Oh, M. S. (2017). *Use of traditional herbal medicine as an alternative in dental treatment in Mexican dentistry: a review.* Pharmaceutical Biology, 55(1), 1992–1998. https://doi.org/10.1080/13880209.2017.1347188

D'Alberto, A. (n.d.). *Chinese herbal medicine - benefits and safety.* Dr (TCM) Attilio D'Alberto. https://www.attiliodalberto.com/chinese-herbal-medicine/

Dallmeier, L. (n.d.). *How to make macerated oils.* Formula Botanica. https://formulabotanica.com/how-to-make-macerated-oils/

Dantoft, T., Andersson, L., Nordin, S., & Skovbjerg, S. (2015). *Chemical Intolerance. Current Rheumatology Reviews*, 11(2), 167–184. https://doi.org/10.2174/1573397111102150702111101

Davis, J. (2019, November 11). *Harvesting and preserving herbs for the home gardener.* NC State Extension Publications. https://content.ces.ncsu.edu/harvesting-and-preserving-herbs-for-the-home-gardener

Delight in dandelion. (2017, May 22). *Tea Mind Today by the Republic of Tea.* https://the.republicoftea.com/tea-library/herbal-tea-and-tisanes/delight-in-dandelion/

Diarrhea (holistic). (2015, June 8). Peace Health. https://www.peacehealth.org/medical-topics/id/hn-1203008#hn-1203008-supplements

Diuretics. (2021, August 13). Mayo Clinic. https://www.mayoclinic.org/diseases-conditions/high-blood-pressure/in-depth/diuretics/art-20048129

Dosage and dosage forms in herbal medicine. (2015, June 23). IKnowledge. https://clinicalgate.com/dosage-and-dosage-forms-in-herbal-medicine/

Douglas, J. (2021, May 6). *Ethical foraging- Responsibility and reciprocity.* Organic Growers School. https://organicgrowersschool.org/ethical-foraging-responsibility-and-reciprocity/

Drying: Herbs. (n.d.). National Center for Home Food Preservation. https://nchfp.uga.edu/how/dry/herbs.html

Ellis, M. E. (2020, July 16). *How to harvest herbs – General tips for picking herbs.* Gardening Know-How. https://www.gardeningknowhow.com/edible/herbs/hgen/general-tips-for-picking-herbs.htm

Ethnobotany - Historical use by Native Americans. (n.d.). Bighorn

Botanicals, Inc. https://bighornbotanicals.com/ethnobotany

Feverfew. (2020, December). National Center for Complementary and Integrative Health. https://www.nccih.nih.gov/health/feverfew

5 herbs for memory boost and concentration. (2020, October 15). The Guardian Nigeria. https://guardian.ng/life/5-herbs-for-memory-boost-and-concentration/

Fletcher, J. (2019, January 10). *Herbal tinctures: 6 types and recipes* (D. R. Wilson, Ed.). Medical News Today. https://www.medicalnewstoday.com/articles/324149#benzoin

Fletcher, J. (2020, January 12). *Nine ways to raise blood pressure* (C. Stephens, Ed.). Medical News Today. https://www.medicalnewstoday.com/articles/319506#natural-ways-to-raise-blood-pressure

Foraging laws. (n.d.). Forage Culture. https://www.forageculture.com/foraging-laws

Fotsing Yannick Stéphane, F., Kezetas Jean Jules, B., El-Saber Batiha, G., Ali, I., & Ndjakou Bruno, L. (2021). Extraction of bioactive compounds from medicinal plants and herbs. *Pharmacognosy - Medicinal Plants [Working Title].* https://doi.org/10.5772/intechopen.98602

Gardiner, B. (2021, February 14). *9 basic principles of ethical wildcrafting for beginners.* The Outdoor Apothecary. https://www.outdoorapothecary.com/ethical-wildcrafting/

Garner-Wizard, M., Henson, S., Hoots, D., Robbins, S., & Van De Walle, G. (2006, August 15). *Herbs in the treatment of back pain* (T. Brendler, M. Henshaw, K. McPhee, B. Quintana, C. Waterman, M. Blumenthal, & L. Glenn, Eds.). American Botanical Council. https://www.herbalgram.org/resources/herbclip/issues/bin_310/review44523/

Gersie, B. (2018, June 21). *An amateur's intro to fungi & mushroom foraging.* The Flying Pan. https://theflyingpan.co.za/an-amateurs-intro-to-funghi-mushroom-foraging/

Glycyrrhiza lepidota - American licorice. (n.d.). Native Plant Trust: Go Botany. https://gobotany.nativeplanttrust.org/species/glycyrrhiza/lepidota/

Goldenseal. (2021, March). National Center for Complementary and Integrative Health. https://www.nccih.nih.gov/health/goldenseal

Gray, A. (n.d.). *Nicotiana clevelandii.* SEINet Arizona - New Mexico Chapter. https://swbiodiversity.org/seinet/taxa/index.php?taxon=3889&clid=3575

Halder, S., Anand, U., Nandy, S., Oleksak, P., Qusti, S., Alshammari, E. M., El-Saber Batiha, G., Koshy, E. P., & Dey, A. (2021). *Herbal drugs and natural bioactive products as potential therapeutics: A review on pro-cognitives and brain boosters perspectives.* Saudi Pharmaceutical Journal : SPJ, 29(8), 879–907.

https://doi.org/10.1016/j.jsps.2021.07.003

Hanes, E. (2020, March 25). *Natural ways to raise low blood pressure* (W. C. Lloyd III, Ed.). Healthgrades. https://www.healthgrades.com/right-care/symptoms-and-conditions/natural-ways-to-raise-low-blood-pressure

Heger, E. (2020, August 19). *4 of the best natural supplements and herbs for depression.* Insider. https://www.insider.com/guides/health/mental-health/natural-remedies-for-depression

Herbal medicine. (n.d.). Merriam Webster. https://www.merriam-webster.com/dictionary/herbal%20medicine

Herbal medicines. (2021, November 23). NHS. https://www.nhs.uk/conditions/herbal-medicines/

Herbs and Supplements for boils and abscesses. (n.d.). Complimentary and Alternative Medicine; St. Luke's Hospital. Retrieved September 26, 2022, from https://www.stlukes-stl.com/health-content/medicine/33/002402.htm

Herbs and supplements that improve circulation. (2017, May 22). Incredible Veins. https://incredibleveins.com/herbs-supplements-improve-circulation/

Herbs for indigestion. (n.d.). Natural Eye Care. https://www.naturaleyecare.com/health-conditions/indigestion/indigestion-herbs.asp

Herrera, H. (n.d.). *Fresh vs dried herbs and ground vs whole spices.* Webstaurant Store Blog. https://www.webstaurantstore.com/blog/2660/fresh-vs-dried-herbs.html

High blood sugar (hyperglycaemia). (2022, May 27). NHS. https://www.nhs.uk/conditions/high-blood-sugar-hyperglycaemia/

Higuera, V. (2019, July 6). *What are the possible benefits of lavender? The must-know facts about the therapeutic plant* (K. Kennedy, Ed.). Everyday Health. https://www.everydayhealth.com/diet/what-are-possible-benefits-lavender-must-know-facts-about-therapeutic-plant/

How to freeze fresh herbs. (2022, August 26). Life Made Simple. https://lifemadesimplebakes.com/how-to-freeze-fresh-herbs/

How to make essential oils. (n.d.). Nourished Essentials. https://nourishedessentials.com/blogs/healthwellness/how-to-make-essential-oils

Hydrangea cinerea. (n.d.-a). North Carolina Extension Gardener Plant Toolbox; North Carolina State University Extension. https://plants.ces.ncsu.edu/plants/hydrangea-cinerea/

Hydrangea cinerea. (n.d.-b). Encyclopedia of Medicinal Plants. https://wiki.medicinalplants-uses.com/index.php/Hydrangea_cinerea

Hydrangea cinerea — ashy hydrangea. (n.d.). Native Plant Trust: Go Botany. https://gobotany.nativeplanttrust.org/species/hydrangea/cinerea/

Hyperglycemia (high blood sugar). (2020, February 11). Cleveland Clinic. https://my.clevelandclinic.org/health/diseases/9815-hyperglycemia-high-blood-sugar

Ipomopsis longiflora. (2007, January 1). Lady Bird Johnson Wildflower Center; The University of Texas at Austin. https://www.wildflower.org/plants/result.php?id_plant=iplo2

Isbill, J., Kandiah, J., & Kružliaková, N. (2020). *Opportunities for health promotion: Highlighting herbs and spices to improve immune support and well-being.* Integrative Medicine (Encinitas, Calif.), 19(5), 30–42. https://www.ncbi.nlm.nih.gov/pmc/articles/PMC7815254/

Jabbour, N. (n.d.). *How to harvest herbs: How and when to harvest homegrown herbs.* Savvy Gardening. https://savvygardening.com/how-to-harvest-herbs/

Jeanroy, A. (2020, October 9). *How to use a food dehydrator to dry herbs.* The Spruce Eats. https://www.thespruceeats.com/use-a-food-dehydrator-dry-herbs-1762397

Jenkins, L. (2021, October 27). *5 herbs for menstrual cramps & period symptoms.* The Herbal CommitTea. https://herbalcommittea.com/blogs/news/5-herbs-for-menstrual-cramps-period-symptoms

Jiang, C., Yuan, Y., Yang, G., Jin, Y., Liu, L., Zhao, Y., & Huang, L. (2016). *Fluorescence visual detection of herbal product substitutions at terminal herbal markets by CCP-based FRET technique.* Scientific Reports, 6(1). https://doi.org/10.1038/srep35540

Johnson, J. (2018, July 30). *9 herbal teas for relieving constipation* (D. R. Wilson, Ed.). Medical News Today. https://www.medicalnewstoday.com/articles/322624#nine-herbal-teas-for-constipation

Johnson, J. (2020, March 6). *What to know about terpenes* (E. Theisen, Ed.). Medical News Today. https://www.medicalnewstoday.com/articles/what-are-terpenes

Kaefer, C. M., & Milner, J. A. (2011). *Chapter 17: Herbs and spices in cancer prevention and treatment.* In I. F. F. Benzie & S. Wachtel-Galor (Eds.), Herbal medicine: Biomolecular and clinical aspects - 2nd edition. CRC Press/Taylor & Francis. https://www.ncbi.nlm.nih.gov/books/NBK92774/

Keating, H. (2018, October 29). *Foraging in October: which wild mushrooms can you eat?* Woodland Trust. https://www.woodlandtrust.org.uk/blog/2018/10/foraging-in-autumn-wild-mushrooms/

Kendle. (2018, September 14). *How to make herbal infusions & decoctions for wellness support.* Mountain Rose Herbs. https://blog.mountainroseherbs.com/herbal-infusions-and-decoctions

Kenson, L. (n.d.). *Herb bombs / How to freeze fresh herbs in olive oil.* Free Your Fork. https://www.freeyourfork.com/how-to-freeze-fresh-herbs-in-olive-oil/

Kester, S. (2021, September 8). *10+ celebrities who prefer to use natural medicine.* Diply. https://diply.com/151060/10-celebrities-who-prefer-to-use-natural-medicine

Kilham, C. (2015, October 26). *Rosy periwinkle: A life saving plant.* Fox News. https://www.foxnews.com/health/rosy-periwinkle-a-life-saving-plant

Kloos, S. (n.d.). *Wildcrafting basics: Ethical wildcrafting.* The School of Forest Medicine. https://forestmedicine.net/ecological-intelligence-blog/2017/4/10/ethical-wildcrafting

Kubala, J. (2020, October 5). *The 10 best herbs to boost energy and focus* (A. Richter, Ed.). Healthline. https://www.healthline.com/nutrition/herbs-for-energy#1.-Ginseng

Kurek, J. (Ed.). (2019). *Introductory chapter.* In *Alkaloids - Their importance in nature and human life.* Intech Open. https://doi.org/10.5772/intechopen.85400

La Forge, T. (2021, December 10). *How to use herbs for anxiety and stress* (K. Marengo, Ed.). Healthline. https://www.healthline.com/health/mental-health/herbs-for-stress-recipe

LaVolpe, N. (2021, March 25). *10 natural ways to treat a fever.* Farmers' Almanac. https://www.farmersalmanac.com/10-natural-ways-treat-fever-26657

Li, J., Bai, L., Wei, F., Zhao, J., Wang, D., Xiao, Y., Yan, W., & Wei, J. (2019). *Therapeutic Mechanisms of Herbal Medicines Against Insulin Resistance: A Review.* Frontiers in Pharmacology, 10. https://doi.org/10.3389/fphar.2019.00661

Licher, C. (n.d.). *Aromatherapy article: Desert lavender (Hyptis emoryi) essential oil.* Phibee Aromatics. https://phibeearomatics.com/aromatherapy-article-desert-lavender.html

Lipoproteins. (2022, May 22). Cleveland Clinic. https://my.clevelandclinic.org/health/articles/23229-lipoprotein

Long, J. (2022, March 4). *Ashwagandha goes mainstream in U.S. as sales boom.* Natural Products Insider. https://www.naturalproductsinsider.com/ingredients/ashwagandha-goes-mainstream-us-sales-boom

Love Thyself Daily 2020. (2021). *Hummingbird blossom - Native American healing* [Video]. In YouTube. https://www.youtube.com/watch?v=XDVFqmpqfOY

Marciano, Dr. M. (n.d.-a). *Cardiac tonic*. The Naturopathic Herbalist. https://thenaturopathicherbalist.com/herbal-actions/b-d/cardiac-tonic-2/

Marciano, Dr. M. (n.d.-b). *Mucilage*. The Naturopathic Herbalist. https://thenaturopathicherbalist.com/plant-constituents/mucilage/

Martinez, R. (2015, August 25). *Your new favorite microwave hack—Or, why you don't need a dehydrator*. Bon Appétit. https://www.bonappetit.com/test-kitchen/cooking-tips/article/microwave-hack

Mathias, J. (2016, June 24). *The beginners guide to analytical testing: Definitions, pronunciation & applications*. Innovatech. https://www.innovatechlabs.com/newsroom/968/beginners-guide-analytical-testing-definitions-pronunciation-applications/

Mayer, F. L., Wilson, D., & Hube, B. (2013). *Candida albicans pathogenicity mechanisms*. Virulence, 4(2), 119–128. https://doi.org/10.4161/viru.22913

Medical herbs and plants. (n.d.). Godioli & Bellanti. https://www.godioliebellanti.com/medical-herbs-and-plants/?lang=en

Milk thistle. (2020, August). National Center for Complementary and Integrative Health. https://www.nccih.nih.gov/health/milk-thistle

Mustafa, A., & Turner, C. (2011). *Pressurized liquid extraction as a green approach in food and herbal plants extraction: A review*. Analytica Chimica Acta, 703(1), 8–18. https://doi.org/10.1016/j.aca.2011.07.018

Muyumba, N. W., Mutombo, S. C., Sheridan, H., Nachtergael, A., & Duez, P. (2021). Quality control of herbal drugs and preparations: the methods of analysis, their relevance and applications. *Talanta Open*, 4, 100070. https://doi.org/10.1016/j.talo.2021.100070

Myths about herbal medicine. (n.d.). The Apothecary. https://www.google.com/url?q=https://the-apothecary.co.nz/myths-about-herbal-medicine/&sa=D&source=docs&ust=1662988219534820&usg=AOvVaw23WUBPh-tj651opdVEf91L

Native American lavender mythology. (n.d.). Native Languages. http://www.native-languages.org/legends-lavender.htm

Native American Wild Rose Mythology. (n.d.). Native Languages. http://www.native-languages.org/wild-rose.htm

Nazario, B. (2021, June 14). *Alternative treatments for high cholesterol*. WebMD. https://www.webmd.com/cholesterol-management/high-cholesterol-alternative-therapies

Norris, M. (n.d.). *Best Methods for Drying Herbs for Stronger Medicinal Properties*. Melissa K Norris. https://melissaknorris.com/podcast/when_how_harvest_dry_herbs/

Organizaciòn Mundial De La Salud. (2007). *WHO guidelines for assessing quality of herbal medicines with reference to contaminants and residues*. Geneva.

Osefo, N., Ito, T., & Jensen, R. T. (2009). Gastric acid hypersecretory states: Recent insights and advances. *Current Gastroenterology Reports*, 11(6), 433–441. https://doi.org/10.1007/s11894-009-0067-6

Ovenden, S. (n.d.). *Foraging: A beginner's guide*. BBC Good Food. https://www.bbcgoodfood.com/howto/guide/foraging

Parthenium integrifolium — wild feverfew. (n.d.). Native Plant Trust: Go Botany. https://gobotany.nativeplanttrust.org/species/parthenium/integrifolium/

Percolation of herbs. (n.d.). You Are the Healer. https://youarethehealer.org/herbal-medicine/making-herbal-products/percolation-of-herbs/

Petruzzello, M. (2021, February 26). *Labrador tea*. Encyclopedia Britannica. https://www.britannica.com/plant/Labrador-tea

Phlox subulata. (n.d.). Native Plant Trust. https://plantfinder.nativeplanttrust.org/plant/Phlox-subulata

Piccolo, M. (n.d.). *A complete guide on how to store dried herbs*. Drying All Foods. https://dryingallfoods.com/store-dried-herbs/

Pines, G. (2019, July 31). *Open your eyes: A responsible guide to foraging*. FoodPrint. https://foodprint.org/blog/sustainable-foraging/

Plant information: Common name: Sage - California white sage. (n.d.). Mountain Herb Estate Nursery. https://www.herbgarden.co.za/mountainherb/herbinfo.php?id=627

Plant of the month: Frangula californica. (2017, August 11). Valley Water News. https://valleywaternews.org/2017/08/11/plant-of-the-month-frangula-californica/

Premenstrual syndrome (PMS). (n.d.). Mayo Clinic. https://www.mayoclinic.org/diseases-conditions/premenstrual-syndrome/symptoms-causes/syc-20376780?utm_source=Google&utm_medium=abstract&utm_content=Premenstrual-syndrome&utm_campaign=Knowledge-panel

Prevention and treatment of high cholesterol (hyperlipidemia). (2020, November 11). American Heart Association. https://www.heart.org/en/health-topics/cholesterol/prevention-and-treatment-of-high-cholesterol-hyperlipidemia

Prickly pear. (n.d.). Texas beyond History. https://www.texasbeyondhistory.net/coast/nature/images/prickly-pear.html

ProSys Servo Filling Systems. (2016). *HP1200 Herb Press 2016 WEB* [Video]. In YouTube. https://www.youtube.com/watch?v=jbVP77Na82Q&t=87s

Rajak, H. (2020, January 24). *Classification of herbs*. HM Hub. https://hmhub.in/classification-of-herbs/

Raman, R. (2022, August 26). *14 natural ways to improve your insulin sensitivity* (M. Basina, Ed.). Healthline. https://www.healthline.com/nutrition/improve-insulin-sensitivity#TOC_TITLE_HDR_8

Raspberry leaf 101. (2015, July 7). Traditional Medicinals. https://www.traditionalmedicinals.com/articles/plants/raspberry-leaf-101/

Ratini, M. (Ed.). (2021, March 22). *What is homeopathy?* WebMD. https://www.webmd.com/balance/what-is-homeopathy

Rose, S. (2018, June 20). *Harvesting, preparing, and storing edible flowers*. Garden Therapy. https://gardentherapy.ca/harvesting-preparing-and-storing-edible-flowers/

Rouhi-Boroujeni, H., Rouhi-Boroujeni, H., Heidarian, E., Mohammadizadeh, F., & Rafieian-Kopaei, M. (2015). Herbs with anti-lipid effects and their interactions with statins as a chemical anti-hyperlipidemia group drugs: A systematic review. *ARYA Atheroscler*, 11(4), 244–251. PubMed Central. https://www.ncbi.nlm.nih.gov/pmc/articles/PMC4593660/

Saba, H. (2018, May 10). *How to build a nutritive tea*. Herbal Academy. https://theherbalacademy.com/build-nutritive-tea/

Sabandar, C. W., Ahmat, N., Jaafar, F. M., & Sahidin, I. (2013). Medicinal property, phytochemistry and pharmacology of several Jatropha species (Euphorbiaceae): A review. *Phytochemistry*, 85, 7–29. https://doi.org/10.1016/j.phytochem.2012.10.009

Salix exigua. (n.d.). Fire Effects Information System; United States Department of Agriculture. https://www.fs.usda.gov/database/feis/plants/shrub/salexi/all.html

Salix exigua | Coyote willow | Medicinal Uses. (n.d.). Charles W. Kane | Applied Medical Botany. https://medivetus.com/botanic/salix-exigua-coyote-willow-medicinal-uses/

Sandbar willow - Salix exigua. (n.d.). California Native Plant Society: Calscape. https://calscape.org/Salix-exigua-(Sandbar-Willow)?srchcr=sc57f0069499b61

Santos, M. R. V., Moreira, F. V., Fraga, B. P., Souza, D. P. de, Bonjardim, L. R., & Quintans-Junior, L. J. (2011). Cardiovascular effects of monoterpenes: a review. *Revista Brasileira de Farmacognosia*, 21(4), 764–771. https://doi.org/10.1590/s0102-695x2011005000119

Sarudy, B. W. (2020, April 4). *Native American medicinal plant - Hummingbird blossom or buck brush. Native Americans*. https://ournativeamericans.blogspot.com/2020/04/hummingbird-blossom-or-buck-brush.html

School of Natural Medicine programmes. (n.d.). University of the Western Cape. https://www.uwc.ac.za/study/all-areas-of-study/schools/school-of-natural-medicine/programmes

7 natural sore throat remedies. (n.d.). Ear, Nose and Throat Institute. https://entinstitute.com/7-natural-sore-throat-remedies/

7Song. (2019, November 2). *The tincture press.* Northeast School of Botanical Medicine. https://7song.com/the-tincture-press/

Sharma, B. K. (2011, May 31). *Extraction techniques for herbal drugs - Part 1.* Biotech Articles. https://www.biotecharticles.com/Agriculture-Article/Extraction-Techniques-for-Herbal-Drugs-Part-1-907.html

Shi, J., Arunasalam, K., Yeung, D., Kakuda, Y., Mittal, G., & Jiang, Y. (2004). Saponins from edible legumes: chemistry, processing, and health benefits. *Journal of Medicinal Food*, 7(1), 67–78. National Library of Medicine | National Center for Biotechnology Information. https://doi.org/10.1089/109662004322984734

Shrubs of the Adirondacks: American fly honeysuckle (lonicera canadensis). (n.d.). Adirondacks Forever Wild. https://wildadirondacks.org/adirondack-shrubs-american-fly-honeysuckle-lonicera-canadensis.html

Side effects - Chemotherapy. (2020, January 29). NHS. https://www.nhs.uk/conditions/chemotherapy/side-effects/

Side effects of radiation therapy. (2020, July). Cancer.net. https://www.cancer.net/navigating-cancer-care/how-cancer-treated/radiation-therapy/side-effects-radiation-therapy

Solvent. (2017, April 28). Biology Dictionary. https://biologydictionary.net/solvent/

Sons, T. (2016, January 26). *Phlox information & its medicinal uses.* TN Nursery. https://www.tnnursery.net/blog/phlox-information-its-medicinal-uses/

Stannard, K. (2020, August 7). *Invasive of the week: Common mullein.* Matthaei Botanical Gardens and Nichols Arboretum. https://mbgna.umich.edu/invasive-of-the-week-common-mullein/

Stansbury, J. (2017). *Molecular mechanisms of action for the "blood movers" in circulatory disorders.* Southwest conference on botanical medicine. https://www.botanical-medicine.org/Molecular-Mechanisms-of-Action-for-the-Blood-Movers-in-Circulatory-Disorders

Staughton, J. (2021, August 3). *12 surprising medicinal uses of pineappleweed.* Organic Facts. https://www.organicfacts.net/health-benefits/herbs-and-spices/pineappleweed.html

Steckel, L. (n.d.). *Wild garlic.* The University of Tennessee Extension. chrome-extension://efaidnbmnnnibpcajpcglclefindmkaj/https://extension.tennessee.edu/publications/documents/W157.pdf

Stephenson, A. (2019, March 27). *The mysterious powers of American ginseng.* Smithsonian Center for Folklife and Cultural Heritage.

https://folklife.si.edu/magazine/mysterious-medicinal-economic-powers-american-ginseng

Streimikyte, P., Viskelis, P., & Viskelis, J. (2022). Enzymes-assisted extraction of plants for sustainable and functional applications. *International Journal of Molecular Sciences*, 23(4), 2359. https://doi.org/10.3390/ijms23042359

Sturgeon, S. (2012, February). *Herb identification and authentication.* Mayway. https://www.mayway.com/articles/herb-identification-and-authentication

Tanya. (2022, April 14). *The best ways to use dried herbs.* My Forking Life. https://www.myforkinglife.com/how-to-use-dried-herbs/

Telkamp, M. (n.d.). *4 ways to freeze fresh herbs.* HGTV. https://www.hgtv.com/outdoors/gardens/garden-to-table/4-ways-to-freeze-fresh-herbs

10 tips for wildcrafting herbs. (2015, September 29). Herbal Academy. https://theherbalacademy.com/10-tips-for-wildcrafting-medicinal-herbs/

Tesfaigzi, Y. (2008). Regulation of mucous cell metaplasia in bronchial asthma. *Current Molecular Medicine*, 8(5), 408–415. https://doi.org/10.2174/156652408785160961

Thompson Coon, J. M., & Ernst, E. (2003). Herbs for serum cholesterol reduction: a systematic review. *J Fam Pract*, 52(6), 468–478. National Library of Medicine: National Centre of Biotechnology Information. https://www.ncbi.nlm.nih.gov/books/NBK70118/

Tilley, N. (2022, February 19). *How to dry herbs – Various methods.* Gardening Know-How. https://www.gardeningknowhow.com/edible/herbs/hgen/how-to-dry-herbs-various-methods.htm

Tolsma, M. (n.d.). *Fermentation lids: A complete review.* Bumblebee Apothecary. https://bumblebeeapothecary.com/fermentation-lids/

Top 7 herbs for lung health and respiratory support. (2022, January 25). Organic India. https://organicindiausa.com/blog/herbs-for-lung-health/

2 ways to ferment fresh herbs. (n.d.). Joybilee® Farm. https://joybileefarm.com/2-ways-fermented-fresh-herbs/

Unani Tibb. (n.d.). The School of Health. https://www.schoolofhealth.com/be-better/natural-health-definitions/unani-tibb/

Uva Ursi. (n.d.-a). Gaia Herbs. https://www.gaiaherbs.com/blogs/herbs/uva-ursi

Uva ursi. (n.d.-b). Mount Sinai. https://www.mountsinai.org/health-library/herb/uva-ursi

Uva ursi. (2015, March 24). Kaiser Permanente. https://wa.kaiserpermanente.org/kbase/topic.jhtml?docId=hn-2178007

Valerian. (2020, October). National Center for Complementary and Integrative Health. https://www.nccih.nih.gov/health/valerian

Vestal, P. A. (1952). The ethnobotany of the Ramah Navaho. *Papers of the Peabody Museum of American Archaeology and Ethnology*, 40(4), 40. Native American Ethnobotany Database.

Vickers, A., & Zollman, C. (1999). ABC of complementary medicine: herbal medicine. *BMJ (Clinical Research Ed.)*, 319(7216), 1050–1053. https://doi.org/10.1136/bmj.319.7216.1050

Visser, M. (2015, January 7). *How to source quality herbs.* Growing up Herbal. https://growingupherbal.com/source-quality-herbs/

Wagner, G. D. (2021, November 30). *"Can I eat that?" Answer the question with the universal edibility test.* Backpacker. https://www.backpacker.com/skills/universal-edibility-test/

Wang, C. (2019, May 9). *Yin-Yang in Traditional Chinese Medicine.* Acupuncture and Massage College. https://www.amcollege.edu/blog/yin-and-yang-in-traditional-chinese-medicine

Wegener, T. (n.d.). Devil's claw: From African traditional remedy to modern analgesic and antiinflammatory. *Herbalgram*, 50, 47–54. American Botanical Council. Retrieved August 27, 2022, from https://www.herbalgram.org/resources/herbalgram/issues/50/table -of-contents/article2285/

Welcome to herbal safety. (n.d.). The University of Texas at El Paso. https://www.utep.edu/herbal-safety/

West, H. (2019, September 30). *What are essential oils, and do they work?* Healthline. https://www.healthline.com/nutrition/what-are-essential-oils#how-they-work

What are fermentation weights? Do you need them for your ferments? (n.d.). Preserve & Pickle. https://preserveandpickle.com/what-are-fermentation-weights-do-you-need-them-for-your-ferments/

What is cholesterol. (2020, November 6). American Heart Association. https://www.heart.org/en/health-topics/cholesterol/about-cholesterol

What is menopause? (n.d.). NIH: National Institute on Aging. https://www.nia.nih.gov/health/what-menopause

White, K. (n.d.). *Collecting and saving seeds from herbs.* The Herb Exchange. https://theherbexchange.com/collecting-and-saving-seeds-from-herbs/

Wild ginger. (n.d.). St. Olaf Collegg. https://wp.stolaf.edu/naturallands/forest/ephemerals/wildginger/

Wild rose medicine.* (2021, June 17). Northeast Organic Farming Association: Massachusetts Chapter. https://www.nofamass.org/articles/2021/06/wild-rose-medicine/

Willow. (n.d.). Medicinal Herb Info. http://medicinalherbinfo.org/000Herbs2016/1herbs/willow/

Wong, C. (2022, January 5). *4 herbs to relieve menstrual cramps.* Verywell Health. https://www.verywellhealth.com/herbs-for-menstrual-cramps-89901

Wynia, R. (n.d.). *American liquorice. United States Department of Agriculture: Natural Resources Conservation Service.* chrome-extension://efaidnbmnnnibpcajpcglclefindmkaj/https://www.nrcs.usda.gov/Internet/FSE_PLANTMATERIALS/publications/kspmcpg7571.pdf

Yazawa, M. (2020, July 20). *You have to try this genius TikTok hack for de-stemming herbs.* Real Simple. https://www.realsimple.com/food-recipes/cooking-tips-techniques/tiktok-hack-for-herbs

Zhang, Q.-W., Lin, L.-G., & Ye, W.-C. (2018). Techniques for extraction and isolation of natural products: a comprehensive review. *Chinese Medicine*, 13(1). https://doi.org/10.1186/s13020-018-0177-x

FREE BONUS FROM HBA: EBOOK BUNDLE

Greetings!

First of all, thank you for reading our books. As fellow passionate readers of History and Mythology, we aim to create the very best books for our readers.

Now, we invite you to join our VIP list. As a welcome gift, we offer the History & Mythology Ebook Bundle below for free. Plus you can be the first to receive new books and exclusives! Remember it's 100% free to join.

Simply scan the QR code to join.

OTHER BOOKS BY
HISTORY BROUGHT ALIVE

Available now in Ebook, Paperback, Hardcover, and Audiobook in all regions.

For Kids:

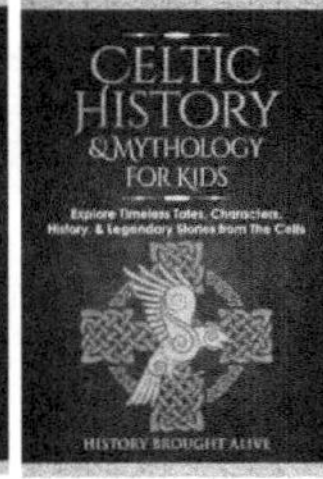

NATIVE AMERICAN WISDOM

We sincerely hope you enjoyed our new book *"Native American Wisdom"*. We would greatly appreciate your feedback with an honest review at the place of purchase.

First and foremost, we are always looking to grow and improve as a team. It is reassuring to hear what works, as well as receive constructive feedback on what should improve. Second, starting out as an unknown author is exceedingly difficult, and Amazon reviews go a long way toward making the journey out of anonymity possible. Please take a few minutes to write an honest review.

Best regards,

History Brought Alive

http://historybroughtalive.com/